EAST ASIA: HISTORY, POLITICS, SOCIOLOGY, CULTURE

edited by
EDWARD BEAUCHAMP
UNIVERSITY OF HAWAII

D1520485

A ROUTLEDGE SERIES

GENDER, ETHNICITY, MARKET FORCES, AND COLLEGE CHOICES

Observations of Ethnic Chinese in Korea

SHEENA CHOI

ROUTLEDGE
A MEMBER OF THE TAYLOR & FRANCIS GROUP
NEW YORK & LONDON/2001

Published in 2001 by
Routledge
A member of the Taylor & Francis Group
29 West 35th Street
New York, NY 10001

10 9 8 7 6 5 4 3 2 1

*Library of Congress Cataloging-in-Publication Data is available from
the Library of Congress.*

ISBN 0-8153-4030-3

Printed on acid-free, 250 year-life paper
Manufactured in the United States of America

Table of Contents

List of Figures

List of Tables

Acknowledgments

It has been an eventful journey from the time I began my graduate studies a number of years ago to this moment. This book, the product of that time and work, represents the realization of a humble but ambitious goal.

I would like to dedicate this book to my children - my lifelines Donald and Katherine. They shouldered the burdens and stress of my journey while keeping me focused on my goal.

I have been blessed with the guidance and support of many professors and friends at SUNY Buffalo. I would like to acknowledge Dr. Maxine Seller who inspired me to take on this project and Dr. Park Enkyung for her groundbreaking work on ethnic Chinese in Korea, which became the initial basis for understanding of the topic. I was exceedingly fortunate to be endowed with the guidance, counsel and support of Dr. William Cummings, Dr. Stephen Jacobson, and Dr. D. Bruce Johnstone. I also gratefully acknowledge the support of Drs. Gay Garland Reed and Edward Bauchamp. I thank Dr. Kathleen Murphey for her friendship, collegiality, and academic mentoring. I want to express my gratitude to the members of the Korean-Huaqiao community who graciously supported this work by sharing their stories. I especially am indebted to Mr. Tan Tao-ching, Mr. Sun Su-yi, Mr. Wang Jie-sun, Mr. Tang Jia-bon, Mr. Wang Ching-ho, and Ryu Sun-pu for their support.

Finally, I thank Dean Roberta Wiener and my new Indiana University-Purdue University Fort Wayne family for continued support.

Abstract

This study is about Korea's ethnic Chinese population and the factors influencing their educational choices, especially of higher education. Physically indistinguishable, the ethnic Chinese in Korea comprise only 0.5% of the entire population, and, due to strict patrilineal citizenship policies, have been unable to attain citizenship. In the past, their children were educated in ethnic schools which prepared them to study in Taiwanese universities. In more recent years the trend in college choice has changed with a majority of the graduates of Chinese ethnic secondary schools entering Korean universities.

Why has there been a shift in educational choice among the ethnic Chinese students in Korea (Korean-Huaqiaos) from predominantly preferring Taiwanese universities in the past to a current preference for Korean universities? This study sought to answer that question by investigating the causes and the extent of the shift in educational choice among the Korean-Huaqiaos from historical, social, policy, and comparative perspectives.

Documents from governmental and academic sources were used for trend and policy analysis. Questionnaires were distributed to senior students at the Seoul Overseas Chinese High School (SOCHS) to understand university preference as well as their perceptions of Korean and Taiwanese societies. The results of document analysis and the information gathered from the questionnaires were used in in-depth interviews with students, parents, teachers, and alumni of SOCHS, and Seoul Huaqiao community leaders to understand why this shift occurred and its impact on the Korean-Huaqiao community.

The research revealed that college choice of Korean-*Huaqiao* changed in relation to 1) the political and legal status of this minority population in the Korean society, 2) changing political realities and social perceptions, 3) varying access to educational opportunities, 4) community pressure, 5) gender, and 6) the increasing or diminishing power of ethnic identity.

This study's findings contribute to the issue of college choice by asserting that decisions made by ethnic communities can have an enormous impact on individual choice; a point which has not been acknowledged in the research about college choice.

Chapter One

Introduction

Problem Statement

In modern society, education is often seen as a vehicle of social mobility. While the myth of social mobility through education may be exaggerated, the value of schooling for socioeconomic attainment is well established (Olneck, 1995). Especially for immigrant children, schooling has been considered "an avenue out of poverty and into the middle class" (Olneck, 1995, p. 322).

Guskin (1965, p. 151) notes "The effect of the school on the identity, attitudes and aspirations of the students is quite understandable" for "almost every society, the educational institutions represent the major socialization institutions for youth. At an age when individuals are most susceptible to alterations in their identity, the school presents a rather consistent picture of desired behaviors. Also, the school is the major agency of society for training in new skills and areas of knowledge which will enable the adolescent to adapt to the larger society." Schools thus take over from the family the socializing function. Assimilation which is an element of socialization "refers to the process whereby one group, usually a subordinate one, becomes indistinguishable from another group, usually a dominant one" (Feinberg and Soltis, 1992, p. 25). Therefore, schooling has historically presented and continues to present a challenge to the values and heritage of immigrant groups (Olneck, 1995). The dilemma of whether to assimilate or to maintain an ethnic identity has had profound consequences for immigrant families, often disrupting relationships between generations by transforming the cultural values, practices, and identities of each generation. For this reason, the schooling process sometimes becomes a source of tension, discomfort, and conflict between first-generation immigrants and their native-born offspring. In less developed societies, even primary level education can result in a separation between children and parents, while in developed societies, such as the United States, Western Europe, and Korea, higher education opens the door to a profession, thus, social mobility. In certain respects, these same attitudes influence educational choices, especially those regarding higher education, made by ethnic Chinese in Korea.

The schooling of immigrants and ethnic minorities thus holds substantial "symbolic power" (Olneck, 1995, p. 310) for both the majority population and its minorities, as it reflects the historical context and the philosophy that inform a given society. In the case of ethnic minorities, the relationship between schooling and cultural values is even more complex, for education often acts as a homogenizing force to integrate immigrant youth into the mainstream language and culture. For this reason, "research on immigrants and education illuminates important societal beliefs and aspirations, prevailing educational policies and practices, and contentious debates about multiculturalism" (Olneck, 1995). In the case of the United States, which is a heterogeneous society, educators' responses to immigrants in the early part of the twentieth century led to the notion of "Americanization" as the goal of education for immigrants. They "thought to promote cultural conformity in order to integrate the population and to enhance immigrants participation in national life" (Olneck, 1995, p. 312).

Korea, which has very small numbers of minorities, is a unique case because it is known as one of the most homogeneous societies in the world. The ethnic Chinese who arrived in Korea at the turn of the twentieth century represent the single largest ethnic minority group, comprising less than one percent of the total Korean population. The title "invisible minority" refers to several elements: small population and indistinguishable physical characteristics with the host population, which make them able to blend into the host society more easily if one chooses, than racially different groups, such as African-Americans in the US. Although ethnic Chinese in Korea have not been traumatized from the dominant society, this minority population's invisibility stands out in their preclusion from the political and economic arena of Korean society.

The ethnic Chinese in Korea calls himself or herself *Han-Hua*, which means Korean-Chinese or simply Huaqiao. In this study I will use the English and Chinese term Korean-Chinese, Huaqiao, and Korean-Huaqiao interchangeably. There are numerous way to spell "Overseas Chinese" and Huaqiao(s). For my purpose, I will use "Overseas Chinese" and Huaqiao(s), which may differ from others' spelling of these words.

Following the Korean War (1950-1953), the ethnic Chinese were unable to return home to China and, at the same time, there was no fresh influx of immigrants to Korea. Thus, the majority of ethnic Chinese in Korea belong to the generation of those who were born and grew up in Korea.

Korea is an "economic miracle" that has achieved an incredible record of growth. Three decades ago its GDP per capita was comparable with that of the poorer countries of Africa and Asia, such as Ghana and Indonesia. Beginning in 1962, however, Korea launched a series of five-year economic development plans, resulting in Korea's emergence as one of the leaders among developing countries as it has become more urban and industrialized. Today its GDP per capita is eight times India's, fifteen times North Korea's, and is already comparable with the weaker economies of the European Union (*CIA World Fact Book*, 1998). Economic strength has enabled Korea to successfully host the Asian Games in 1986, the Olympics in 1988, and the Taejon EXPO '93. Korea has also elected to co-host the 2002 World Cup with Japan. All of these events demonstrate remarkable political, economic, social, and cultural progress. Korean education has also experienced extraordinary growth: quantitative expansion from the 1960s through the 1970s and qualitative development in the 1980s. This growth in education is credited as the driving force behind Korea's national progress and growing international prestige, producing the workforce needed for industrialization and democratization.

Korea's rising economic power has had a significant impact on the relationship between the ethnic Chinese and the larger society. When Korea was a colonized nation and economically underdeveloped, the more affluent ethnic Chinese remained aloof from Korean society. But as the economy developed and the nation grew politically more stable, this minority group could no longer maintain its separateness but rather sought to develop stronger ties with the larger community.

Rapid economic growth is often followed by an influx of immigrants (e.g. guest workers in Western Europe), and, in most cases, the second generation decides to stay in the host nation. However, in Korea the minority ethnic Chinese population decreased during the prosperous period of the 1970s through the 1980s (see figure 1).

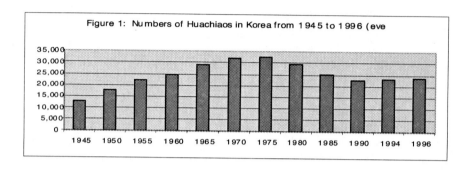

Figure 1: Numbers of Huachiaos in Korea from 1945 to 1996 (eve

According to the Korean Ministry of Justice's *1996 Annual Report of Statistics on Legal Migration*, there are 23,282 ethnic Chinese residing in Korea as legal aliens. Moreover, many ethnic Chinese in Korea believe that about 7,000 to 8,000 resident Chinese people in Korea are floating members, residing elsewhere but keeping resident alien status in Korea. Thus, the actual number of ethnic Chinese in Korea is approximately 15,000, with some estimates as low as 10,000 (*The Economist*, 1996). One study claims that Korea had the greatest loss of its ethnic Chinese population (seven percent) during the 1980s (Poston Jr., Mao, & Yu, 1994), with the result that there was a decrease of more than fifty percent since the 1970s (*Kukmin Daily*, Aug. 24, 1992). This population decrease was due to Chinese emigration rather than to the effects of low fertility or high mortality. Rather than entering Korean universities, ethnic Chinese students opted for Taiwanese universities upon graduation from their ethnic secondary schools. Admission to Taiwanese universities was often utilized as a way to emigrate to Taiwan: it was an opportunity to settle in Taiwan and bring over the remaining family members from Korea upon graduation. The ethnic Chinese in Korea claim that various adverse political and economic forces have led to emigration of the Chinese population from the host country (see figure 2). Further, the majority of ethnic Chinese in Korea has been vague about staying in Korea, while strongly defining themselves by their ethnic identity.

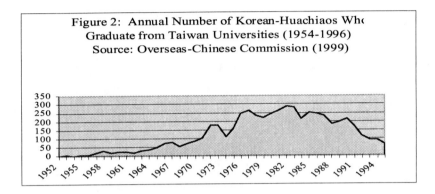

Figure 2: Annual Number of Korean-Huachiaos Who Graduate from Taiwan Universities (1954-1996) Source: Overseas-Chinese Commission (1999)

Such a trend began to reverse during the Seoul Olympics of 1988, and as a result, at present, approximately seventy percent of ethnic Chinese students upon graduation from ethnic secondary schools prefer to study in Korean universities as opposed to Taiwanese universities (see table 1).

Table 1: Seoul Overseas Chinese High School (SOCHS) Seniors in Taiwanese University Track and Korean University Track

Source: SOCHS 1998

Year	Taiwanese University Track Student Numbers (%)	Korean University Track Student Numbers (%)	Total Student Numbers (%)
1992	68 (54)	59 (46)	127 (100)
1993	75 (49)	79 (51)	154 (100)
1994	63 (46)	75 (54)	138 (100)
1995	62 (47)	69 (53)	131 (100)
1996	61 (41)	86 (59)	147 (100)
1997	108 (64)	170 (64)	170 (100)

Students who apply to Korean universities are exempted from taking competitive entrance examinations, as Korean students must. Although the Chinese claim that they experience discrimination in employment opportunities, they are now choosing to stay in Korea after graduation. While more business opportunities have developed in China and there are more possibilities to travel abroad, including to the United States, Taiwan, and China, not many Korean-Chinese have resettled in China and elsewhere. The Chinese population in Korea is stabilizing, a trend that coincides with the increasing enrollment in Korean institutions of higher education.

Therefore, the concept of college choice has largely two meanings: the choice of individuals, which has the more conventional meaning in US literature; and the choice of minority communities, which shapes their decision regarding special schools for their children. The shift in Korean-Chinese students' preference for Korean rather than Taiwanese universities may reflect their changes in perceptions on both the individual and community level (e.g. improved opportunities such as fewer political constraints, better economic incentives, and stronger social networks for the ethnic Chinese in Korea). This study will illuminate the impact of these political and social changes by focusing on the overarching question, "Why has there been a shift in the choice of higher education among the ethnic Chinese in Korea?" The following sub-questions were asked in order to answer the main research question:

1.   What is the state of majority/minority relations in Korea, and how does this relationship influence ethnic Chinese students' college choices?
2.   How does community choice influence individual choice?
3.   What were the Korean government's social, economic, and educational policies toward the ethnic Chinese since 1945, and how did these policies influence this minority's educational choices?
4.   What are the advantages and disadvantages of studying in Korean and Taiwanese universities?
5.   To what extent have Chinese students in Korea chosen Korean over Taiwanese universities?
6.   What do students, parents, teachers, and community leaders think has changed so those students now prefer Korean rather than Taiwanese universities? What are the implications of recent trends?

Comparative, historical, and policy perspectives will deepen the understanding of the changes in the Korean-Huaqiao students' choices in higher education. I employ a comparative perspective to investigate and compare, within a broader spectrum, the experience of the ethnic Chinese in Korea and minorities in other societies. In order to understand the characteristics of the Korean-Huaqiaos, I examine Chinese immigration to Korea from a historical perspective, and consider this phenomenon in light of modern Korean history. I also study the educational, social, and economic policies of the Korean and Taiwanese governments, which have played a critical role in the development of the present relationship between the Koreans and the ethnic Chinese. These various perspectives cannot be examined independently of each other because elements in each area have undeniably influenced the shift in educational choices among the ethnic Chinese in Korea.

Methodology

To deepen one's understanding of this extremely small minority and the rationale for their choices in higher education, both a quantitative methodology, involving survey questionnaires, and a qualitative methodology, involving semi-structured interviews and document analysis, were used in this case study. Documents were collected from the archives of the Seoul Overseas Chinese High School (SOCHS), The Taipei Mission (unofficial diplomatic agent of Taiwan), various Korean newspapers, Korean and Taiwanese government documents, and other academic publications. A survey questionnaire was distributed to the entire senior class of the Seoul Overseas Chinese High School. Located in the capital of Korea, where sixty percent of the ethnic Chinese reside, SOCHS draws students from all over Korea, and thus, this school is composed of a more diverse student population than other regional ethnic Chinese schools. The collection yielded an eighty percent return.

A semi-structured interview was also employed. The purpose of the interviews was to understand ethnic Chinese attitudes toward education in the context of this population's social milieu. Interviews with ten community leaders (including a newspaper editor and publisher, businessmen, physicians, university professors, and employees of Taipei Mission), twelve students, five teachers, ten parents of both Korean university-track and Taiwanese university-track students, ten alumni of SOCHS (five Korean university graduates and five Taiwanese university graduates), and numerous informal contacts with community members were conducted during the month of August 1998. Due to the extremely small size of the ethnic Chinese population in Korea, these samples adequately represent the community.

A second survey of SOCHS seniors was conducted in June 1999 (the same population group as the first survey) to collect more in-depth information. I have chosen SOCHS because of its easy access to me as an alumna, its larger population base, and its diverse student body as compared to other regional Overseas-Chinese schools.

Focus of the Study

The analysis behind this research emphasizes the experiences and perceptions of Korean-Chinese teachers, students, parents, alumni, and community leaders in order to understand their perception of reality and the basis for their choices of institutions of higher education. This research was conceptualized on the premise that the Korean-Chinese's choices of higher education are embedded in social constructions and phenomena, and that these choices should therefore be understood in terms of the Korean-Chinese's attendant social milieu. However, their choices should also be understood in the broader context of Korean and global circumstances and pressures. This research integrated micro and macro levels of analysis, exemplified a socio-cultural approach, and used both quantitative and qualitative research methods that highlighted and brought the "voices" of the participants to bear on an understanding of the educational choices and issues among the ethnic Chinese minority in Korea.

Research in Korea

As one of the world's most homogenous societies, Korea has done very little research into its ethnic minority. In 1986 Park conducted a study about the "Ethnic Identity of Korean-Huaqiaos [*Hankuk Hwakyoyi Zhongjoksung*]," which provides an initial understanding of the topic. Since then, however, very little research about the Korean-Chinese has been carried out. Interpretative research evidence that reveals the realities of the ethnic minority has yet to emerge as there are no ethnographic or qualitative studies showing the interactions and practices of the Korean-Chinese, or illuminating how they interpret their perceived opportunities in a Korean context.

Therefore, it is possible to postulate that there is a need to know what is happening to the ethnic Chinese population within Korea, regardless of the minority's ethnic status and size, in order for the dominant society to provide equitable policies to which all human beings are entitled in this increasingly globalizing world.

Significance of the Study

This study illuminates the ways in which social context shapes students' desire for particular postsecondary institutions. I analyzed the impact of nationality, economics, and educational policies of both the Korean and the Taiwanese governments on the educational choices of the Korean-Chinese. The empirical evidence in this study documents how these policies and the students' perceptions of their opportunities influence their aspirations. I consider ethnicity and gender within the social milieu and the organizational environment in order to examine the larger picture. For example, those who chose Taiwanese universities had a stronger ethnic identity than Korean university-bound students.

The potential contribution of this research lies in the fact that the methodological approach and techniques it uses can be replicated, and that enough useful information has been gathered to provide a perspective on the Korean-Chinese and their rationales for their educational choices in the context of their social milieu. Through a historical and comparative approach this study will bring out the multiple intertwined social, economic, and political forces that shape those choices.

Providing equitable policies based on inalienable human rights for all population groups is a challenge for many multiethnic societies. For a long time, Koreans shed much blood and sweat to attain democracy and improve their quality of life. At a time when Korea is prospering and striving to take its place among the nations of the world, democracy and the quality of life should not be limited to Koreans but extended to its minorities as well. This research will provide another perspective from which to contemplate issues of ethnicity in Korea, that is, within the framework of international ideals and principles. It will provide useful and crucial data to Korean decision and policy-makers, who are in the process of bringing about social reforms. The combination of document analysis, interview, and survey questionnaires can be replicated and tested in other national settings in which a small minority exists within a larger homogeneous society.

Most of all, this research brings out the "voice" of the Korean-Chinese, who are "invisible" and often overlooked in the larger society. As a homogeneous society, Korea lacks awareness of ethnic or multicultural issues. This study will be also a useful tool for the Korean-Chinese community to examine itself. It is my greatest hope that this study will contribute to a mutual understanding between the Korean society at large and its ethnic minority population. It is hoped that this study will expand the horizon of Koreans concerning ethnic and multicultural issues, and also bring about a common understanding between the Korean and the ethnic Chinese populations.

Limitations

Since it is based on a small sample, this study is meant to be explanatory. It has attempted to go beyond the quantitative studies' emphases on the "what" and "how many" kinds of questions, and, instead, focuses on "why" and "how" students make decisions about where to go to college. I chose a qualitative methodology to provide insight into the motivations and behavior of students as they go through the process of selecting a college to find out why students make the choices they do. Through an understanding of a student's rationales for selecting an institution of higher education, educators and policy makers in Korea can devise meaningful and effective policies to address social equity. Given the restrictions of geographic location, and the number and types of schools, the findings of this study cannot be generalized. However, the information and findings of this study can be used to design further research into what influences the college choices of ethnic minorities within larger societies.

Also, there is a certain amount of randomness regarding each individual's consideration of colleges and possibly his or her final choice. However, the specific choices are not as important as the process that the students go through and the set of outcomes they define as acceptable. The school, family, and community all influence college-bound seniors and shape their aspirations and sense of entitlement (McDonough, 1997). Political and social policies affect students' perceptions of the opportunities and education available to them and shape their choices. This study will show how Korean-Huaqiao students make decisions about where to go to college and why that is an important issue of social equity.

Organization of the Study

This study is organized in the following way: Chapter Two presents the literature review. Chapter Three gives details on the methodology. Chapter Four discusses the background of the study (the definition of the Overseas-Chinese and the Korean-Huaqiaos, the demography of the Korean-Huaqiaos and the social and educational history of the Korean-Huaqiaos). Chapter Five presents the historical background of Chinese immigration to Korea and the social and economic history of the Korean-Huaqiaos. Chapter Six explains the Huaqiao education in Korea, the Korean government's educational policies toward the ethnic Chinese in Korea, and its influence on the choice of higher education by this population group. Chapter Seven discusses gender and ethnicity in college choices. Chapter Eight concludes the research.

Chapter Two
Review of Literature

Very few studies have been carried out on the Chinese living in Korea, and no research has been done on their educational system. As a result, in this study, I am assuming that the Chinese face many problems similar to those that minorities confront elsewhere. Therefore, this literature review will look at the issues other minorities deal with concerning ethnic identity, perception of ethnicity, ethnic schools, and related problems such as those faced by the Chinese in Southeast Asia and the Koreans in Japan.

The experience of the Chinese in Korea can be viewed as that of a voluntary minority. We can learn something about how the Chinese have adjusted to the larger Korean culture from the vast literature regarding voluntary minorities in the United States. I will also examine the literature on involuntary minorities, since one aspect of the Chinese experience in Korea is the history of being cut off from the homeland by international politics. For this purpose, I will review the literature on the Koreans in Japan as an example of an involuntary minority, and the Koreans in China and the Chinese in Southeast Asia as an example of a voluntary minority in order to compare the adjustment and adaptation of the ethnic Chinese in Korea.

"Through a complex interactive process involving an individual aspirations and institutional admissions, students connect with colleges. Potential students find out about and enroll in college through the encouragement of family, friends, high school advisors, teachers, private counselors, freeway signs, radio, television, newspaper, direct mail advertising, and many other sources" (McDonough, 1997, p. 1). Where do the ethnic Chinese in Korea go to college and why? This study examines the ways in which geopolitics, ethnicity, curriculum, academic preparation, social milieu, and organizational habitus combine to shape Korean-Huaqiao students' perceptions of their opportunities for a college education as a minority group in Korea.

College Choice Research

Drawing from other studies (Alexander & Eckland, 1975; Hearn, 1991; Karen 1988; Thomas 1979) McDonough, (1997, p. 4) concludes that "for all students, academic achievement remains the most important determinant of whether and where they go to college," adding that "systematic relationships exist within achievement groupings between income and college selectivity." The influence of factors such as socioeconomic background translate into "cultural capital" and "habitus" (Bourdieu, 1977; McDonough et al., 1997; Hearn, 1984; 1991; DiMaggio, 1982), academic achievement (DiMaggio and Powell, 1983; Schurenberg, 1989), individual expectation and motivation (Hearn 1984), and gender (Alexander and Eckland 1977; Hearn 1991). In her multivariate analyses, McDonough (1994, p. 5) suggests "a hierarchy of effects of background characteristics on educational attainment . . . from strongest to weakest, is social class, race, and gender."

It is well established that education not only influences choice of occupation but also social mobility. Richey's (1976) study shows that there is a high tendency for youth to seek alternate opportunities when society limits their occupational aspirations. Featherman and Hauser's (1978) analysis leads us to conclude that education has been an avenue of occupational attainment for immigrant groups. High educational attainment has facilitated the mobility of some immigrant groups, while a lack of schooling has severely impeded the occupational mobility of other groups. In the United States, for example, both foreign-born and second-generation Mexican men suffer an occupational disadvantage on account of their low levels of educational attainment while Russian Jews have achieved greater professional status through high educational attainment (Olneck, 1995). Examining data from the 1976 Survey of Education and Income, Hirshman and Wong (1984) find similar results and conclude that "It is only through over achievement in education that Asian-Americans reach socioeconomic parity with the majority population" (p. 600). In a different context, however, the Korean-Huaqiaos' educational choices which emphasizing ethnic identity rather than learning about the larger Korean society led to a lowered occupational status for them in Korea.

The literature tells us that the process of selecting a college can be a lengthy one that extends back to the earliest inculcation of college aspirations and begins with a broad overview of the post secondary educational opportunities available to students (Chapman, 1981; Hossler, Braxton, and Coopersmith, 1989). Passing through a variety of stages, each student narrows his/her options to a single set of institutions (Hossler and Gallagher, 1987; Jackson, 1982; Litten, 1982). The Hossler model specifies those stages as predisposition, search, and choice. In the predisposition phase, a student first decides whether to attend college. The search phase occurs when the student looks for general information about colleges, forms a choice set, and begins to consider several specific institutions. In the final choice phase, the student narrows the choice set down to a single college and decides to attend that institution (McDonough, 1997).

In students' search and choice phases, a number of factors have been found to be consistently influential: parents, college size, location, academic program, reputation, prestige, selectivity, alumni, peers, friends, and guidance counselor. Availability of financial aid is also important (Hossler, Braxton, and Coopersmity, 1989; Manski and Wise, 1983; Zemsky and Oedel, 1983). Most college choice research focuses on the student's background and the institutional characteristics. According to McDonough,

> While an individual's academic achievement is clearly a key determinant of college attendance, the interplay of a student's social background and the high school's organizational contexts and processes appears central to the question of where an individual attends college (1997, p. 8).

While studies (Alexander and Eckland, 1975; Hearn, 1991; Karen, 1988; Thomas, 1979) report strong linkage between academic achievement and college selection, "systematic relationships exist within achievement groupings between income and college selectivity" (Hearn, 1991). Hearn's (1987) study suggests that upper-income youth are especially likely to enter America's elite colleges. African-Americans, women, and low socio-economic status (SES) students are especially likely to attend less-selective institutions, even if their ability and achievements are high (Hearn, 1984; 1990).

Cultural capital (Bourdieu, 1977) is the property that middle- and upper-class families transmit to their offspring which substitutes for or supplements the transmission of economic capital as a means of maintaining class status and privilege across generations (Bourdieu, 1977a). In other words, middle- and upper-class families highly value a college education and advanced degrees as a means of ensuring continuing economic security, in addition to whatever money or financial assets that can be passed along to their offspring.

The cultural capital theoretical framework of Pierre Bourdieu has been important in many of the new sociological studies that focus on how and why class status plays a role in educational achievement. For the present research I have studied Korean-Huaqiao high school students' college choice processes in their social, cultural, and organizational contexts. And, since most students are admitted to the school which is their first choice, the key issue addressed there is how a student's social-class background and the high school's social and organizational contexts shape a senior's choices about higher education.

Students' educational expectations play a major role in college placement (Hearn, 1984), and oftentimes are the single strongest predictor of four-year college attendance (Thomas, 1980). Long-standing college goals can be resources: intending to go to college increases a student's likelihood of going by twenty-one percent when that intention develops prior to tenth grade, compared to plans formulated during the senior year (Alexander and Cook, 1979). Hearn (1984) contends that students and parents' perceptions, attitudes, and knowledgeability about college attendance may take on distinctive shapes for different social classes and races as early as the tenth grade, and thus may produce differences in a family's college planning. For example, high-SES students tend to take more college preparatory courses.

Multivariate analyses suggest a hierarchy of effects of background characteristics on educational attainment. The order of effects, from strongest to weakest, are social class, race, and gender. Holding achievement constant, race appears to be more influential than gender in affecting the process of college entry (Thomas, 1979). For example, survey data suggests that Asian-Americans have a strong orientation to selective colleges and are twice as likely to apply to the best schools as white students (Karen, 1988). One researcher contends that African-Americans and Hispanics, as a group, are not as likely to try to get into highly selective colleges because of their subjective assessments of the impact of their lower grades, test scores, and levels of participation in extracurricular activities (Karen, 1988).

The most persistent barrier to parity in college entrance is, however, social class background rather than race, ethnicity, or gender (Hearn, 1984; 1991). Social class status exerts twice as much effect on the selectivity of a student's college choice as does ethnicity or gender (Karen 1988). However, gender seems to be significant largely in relation to SES (McDonough, 1997). Earlier research shows that the sorting of women into college destinations is much more strongly affected by their SES background than it is for men (Alexander and Eckland, 1977). However, recent research has documented both some lessening of gender impacts (Hearn, 1991) and the differential conversion capacity of women's educational assets(Persell, Catsambis, and Cookson,

1992). Thus, working-class women are more disadvantaged in educational attainment than are their male counterparts (McDonough, 1997).

The substantial impact of class status on educational attainment operates directly through individual choice and indirectly through the impact of scholastic aptitude on available options (Karen 1988). The ways in which SES affects students' choices is mediated and shaped in part, by "students' and parents' perceptions, attitudes, and knowledgeability about college attendance" (Hearn, 1984 in McDonough, 1997, p. 5). "For example, high SES students tend to take more college preparatory courses" (McDonough, 1997, p. 5).

> A number of differences exist between low-SES, first-generation-college-bound students, and high-SES students whose parents completed college. Students who are first-generation college-bound begin to think about going to college much later than do students whose parents have gone to college, and those thoughts tend to be triggered by school personnel, specifically teachers and counselors (McDonough, 1988; 1997).

> Students whose parents have attended college often get a head start on college preparation in elementary school by taking the right courses and maintaining good grades, and their families convey information to them about the different types of colleges and universities. Meanwhile, first-generation college-bound students do not get this information. Oftentimes they are not taking the right courses and are struggling with the cultural conflicts between their new college-oriented world and the world of their friends, families, and communities (McDonough, 1997).

The issues that are least understood about students' college destinations is the causal process, the web of opportunities, structural arrangements, contingencies, and timing through which school context, SES, and family together shape the process of college planning and choices (Hearn, 1990; 1991). The existing studies of educational attainment emphasize individual attributes as the key determinants of inequalities, largely neglecting the role of educational institutions. However, McDonough (1997, p. 2) asserts that there is need for further study in the areas of "patterns in college access and retention" in organizational contexts as a means to understand the empirical patterns of individual educational outcomes.

The high school environment has a powerful influence on the ways in which students choose colleges. Only two models of college choice, both of which are considerably dated, incorporate the effects of high school context in the shaping of aspirations. Boyle (1966) suggests that college aspirations are influenced not only by individual ability and motivation but also by the imposition of academic standards and the practices of a college-focused high school. Alwin and Otto (1977) offer further insights by differentially analyzing the individual's ability and socioeconomic status levels and the high school's academic standing and socioeconomic status levels.

Research on guidance and counseling indicated that a school, public or private, can affect college plans through an ethos of enabling students. This ethos should be held and acted upon by knowledgeable staff who influence students to specific college preparatory programs (Hotchkiss and Vetter, 1987).

Educational sociologists are now studying how different populations' everyday experiences in and out of school foster recurrent patterns of educational attainment. In addition, for some time now, researchers have been shifting their attention to the growing realization that where a person attends college is critically important to understanding the links between social class and educational attainment, persistence, and occupational achievement (Useem and Karabel, 1986). Differentials in access to particular kinds of institutions are an important aspect of how the educational system contributes to intergenerational transmission of status, since high status students are both more likely to attend college and more likely to attend a good college than are low-status students (Karabel and Astin, 1975).

Ethnic Identity/Ethnic Relations Research

Ogbu (1987; 1991) asserts that minorities are found in "plural societies," those with two or more populations within their respective political boundaries. A population within such a society or nation is a minority group, not because it is numerically smaller, but because it occupies a subordinate power position vis-à-vis another population within the same political boundary. The lesser status has important implications both for the way minorities are treated in various domains of life, including education, and for the way they perceive and respond to events in those areas. Further, Ogbu observes that the way a given minority looks upon and respond to opportunities for schooling depends not only on how they are treated by the dominant group, but also on the terms by which the minorities were initially incorporated into the society. According to Ogbu's "cultural ecological" model, those who joined the society voluntarily – a voluntary minority – seeking better opportunities hold a "dual frame of reference," which "dismisses majority hostility and embraces opportunity." In contrast, involuntary minorities – those who are forced into society through slavery, conquest, or colonization – hold "oppositional" social identities and cultural inversions. They also have pessimistic folk theories of success, which render engagement with the demands of majority institutions a betrayal of group allegiance and collective identity (Olneck, 1995). Therefore, while a voluntary minority views cultural difference as "barriers to be overcome" an involuntary minority sees the "cultural difference they encounter at school as markers of identity to be maintained" (Ogbu, 1987, p. 330). Ogbu's analysis is an interesting framework by which to view the Korean-Huaqiaos, whose status began as a voluntary minority but who were reduced to semi-involuntary status when they could not return to their homeland. Further, the continuous deterioration of their economic status and their lack of political participation within the larger Korean society resemble the characteristics of an involuntary minority.

Johnston (1963, p. 293) defines assimilation as "a process of change during which the immigrant seeks to identify himself in various respects with members of the host group and becomes less distinguishable from them." Drawing from Johnston, Guskin (1968, p. 21) extends the definition to include the fact that an assimilated individual "also accepts their [majority] norms and values and identifies himself with that group [majority]." According to Gordon's (1964) detailed analysis of assimilation, there are three major types of assimilation. The first type is "cultural or behavioral assimilation." Noting assimilation as a "cultural concept" differing from political socialization, Feinberg and Solites (1998) described it as a "process whereby one group, usually a subordinate one, becomes indistinguishable from another group, usually a dominant one" and occurs "As one group takes on the dress, speech patterns, tastes, attitudes, and economic status of the dominant group"(p. 25).

The second type of assimilation is "identification assimilation." Guskin explained that this type of "assimilation is the development of a sense of peoplehood based exclusively on the host society." In this type of assimilation "[t]he individual no longer maintains a separate ethnic identity; the individual's conception of himself becomes similar to that of host culture members and, over time, becomes, the same" (Guskin, p. 22).

A third type of assimilation is "structural assimilation." This type of assimilation involves "a large scale entrance of individuals into cliques, clubs, and institutions of the host society on primary group level" (Guskin, p. 22). According to Gordon, "[o]nce structural assimilation has occurred, either simultaneously with or subsequent to acculturation, all of the other types of assimilation will naturally follow" (p.

81). On the other hand, a structurally unassimilated group "has its own network of cliques, clubs, organizations, and institutions which tend to confine the primary group contacts of its members within the ethnic enclave, while inter-ethnic contacts take place in considerable part only at the secondary group level of employment and the political and civic process" (p. 110-111). The other types of assimilation Gordon pointed out are intermarriage, absence of discrimination, absence of prejudice, absence of value, and power conflict. Building upon Gordon's definitions, Guskin (1968, p. 23) made distinctions "between those individuals who have completely assimilated, and those who share a common national identity with the core culture but have not completely assimilated." There are three specific distinctions:

> Assimilation characterizes individuals who have culturally and behaviorally assimilated, identificationally assimilated, and structurally assimilated. In short, one would not, for the most part, be able to distinguish these people from members of the core culture.
>
> Integration characterizes individuals who have culturally and behaviorally assimilated, who share a common national identity with the majority group but maintain a separate ethnic identity, and who have not structurally assimilated. These people may or may not be the process of assimilating. The extent to which they are is determined by the societal structure and their own group's structure.
>
> Segregation characterizes individuals who have not been assimilated in any manner or at the most have only been culturally or behaviorally assimilated (p. 23).

Guskin pointed out that "in order for individuals who are members of a minority group to *assimilate* into the majority ethnic group they must develop a set of values and behaviors, and sense of nationhood and honored symbols which are the same as the majority group's. Moreover, they must participate in the same primary groups and maintain the same roles as the majority group" (p. 24-25). Guskin (p. 25) quotes from Eisenstadt's (1964) writing of immigrants in Israel:

> . . . the process of absorption, from the point of view of the immigrant's behavior entails the learning of new roles, the transformation of primary group values, and the extension of participation beyond the primary group in the main spheres of society. Only in so far as these processes are successfully coped with are the immi-

grant's concept of himself and his status and his hierarchy of values re-focused into a coherent system, enabling him to become once
more a fully functioning member of society (p. 9)

On the other hand,

For individuals of a minority-ethnic group to be *integrated* into a
society containing a majority ethnic group they must develop a set
of behaviors, a sense of nationhood, and honored symbols which are
the same or very similar to those of the majority group, which
[while] at the same time maintaining their own primary groups and
ethnic identity. While they maintain their own primary groups they
will participate in the employment and/or education of the larger
society (p. 25).

Individuals who are *segregated* do not have a national identity in
common with the majority ethnic group nor do they participate in
the primary groups of the majority or other ethnic groups. They
will have their own separate primary groups, ethnic identity, and
social institutions. While they may participate in the employment
and educational structures (secondary groups) of the larger society
they will do so on the periphery. Often, they will participate in their
own secondary groups (p. 25).

Based on Guskin's analysis, Korean-Huaqiaos are segregated from
Korean society and have the limited option to either remain separate or
assimilate. Since Koreans who control the political machine absolutely
and represent over ninety-nine percent of the nation's total population
will "not readily accept the Chinese as equal members" of Korea, "integration is not an option" (Guskin, p. 25-26). Further, the small size of
the Huaqiao community and its insignificant role in the political and
economic arena make it impossible for them to demand integration.

In *Changing Identity: The Assimilation of Chinese in Thailand*,
Guskin (1968), argue that "Changing the ethnic identity of youth
requires a change in an important element of their conception of themselves—a change in a significant part of their self identity" (p. 27).
Thus, education as a social institution plays an important role in assimilating emigrants into the host country, while at the same time, it can
play a direct role in maintaining ethnic identity (p. 17). The Chinese in
Korea represent a classic example of the latter part of this theory.
Through their own separate educational system, which was sheltered
from Korean influence, the Korean-Huaqiaos maintained a greater
degree of ethnic identity. Further, this firm ethnic identity sustained by
language facility and a familiar educational system induced Huaqiao

students to select Taiwanese universities, a choice that - for those Huaqiaos who remained in Korea - resulted in low morale and maladjustment to their host country.

Nagel notes that ethnic identity is most closely associated with the issues of boundaries (1994). "Culture and history," according to Nagel "are the substance of ethnicity. They are also the basic materials used to construct ethnic meaning. Culture and history are often intertwined in cultural construction" (161). Hobsbawm identifies three functions of traditions: 1) as symbols of group cohesion and membership; 2) to legitimize institutions and authority relations; and 3) "to socialize or inculcate belief, values, or behaviors" (Nagel 1994, p. 163; Hobsbawm 1983, p. 9). Thus, the history and political culture of a particular ethnic group intersect at ethnic identification.

Since the 1980s, "labor market theorists look to political, economic, and historical factors to explain the relationship between ethnic background and educational achievement. They argue that the nature of the history, subordination, and exploitation of a group affects the meanings group members attach to cultural differences. Further, these meanings affect youth's attitudes towards schooling" (Davidson, Yu, and Phelan, 1993, p. 66). For example, according to the researches of Fordam and Ogbu (1986), Ogbu (1987), and Suarez-Orozco (1987) "groups with a longer history of subordination develop an oppositional ethnic identity in which succeeding in school is viewed as selling out to one's oppressors" (Davidson, Yu, and Phelan, 1993, p. 66).

Other bodies of research in ethnicity suggest ethnic identity is "flexible" and "negotiated across time and social situations, rather than received solely from group membership." Furthermore, "Day-to-day social interactions mediate and reshape institutionally-produced social or psychological elements" (Davison, Yu, and Phelan, 1993, p. 67). New groups of scholars challenging the notion of "unchanging ethnic identity grounded in a single shared and agreed upon cultural inventory" (cf. Anzaldua, 1990; Clifford, 1988; Okamura, 1981; Roosens, 1989; Rosaldo, 1989 in Davidson, Yu, and Phelan, 1993, p. 66). These scholars propose that "cultural meanings and practices are dynamic-shifting and often conflictual" (Rosaldo, 1989; Spindler and Spindler, 1990 in Davidson, Yu, and Phelan, 1993, p. 67). Therefore, ethnicity is flexible, socially constructed reality. Ethnic meanings are potentially variable, ethnic boundaries potentially fluid, and ethnic identity constantly recreated, coming forward or retreating to the background in response to the politics and relations that characterize changing social situations. On an individual level, ethnic identity refers to the social presentation of ethnicity in a way that significant others accept and recognize. "Further, ethnic identity depends on how individuals mediate a range of cultural and intercultural phenomena as they seek to establish themselves" (Davidson, Yu, and Phelan, 1993, p. 67). The "Individual may also adopt a bicultural strategy" (Davidson, Yu, and Phelan, 1993, p. 67), "developing a tolerance for contradictions, a tolerance for ambiguity" and an ability to "juggle cultures" (Anzaldua, 1987, p. 79). These beliefs are similar to that of Spindler and Spindler's concepts of "situated self" which is "an adaptation to the immediate realities of modern day life" (Davidson, Yu, and Phelan 1993, p. 67). Ethnicity, therefore, is "socially constructed and therefore potentially flexible" (Davidson, Yu, and Phelan 1993, p. 67).

Research on the Influence of Generational Change

Many studies (Chan, 1987; Rogler, Cooney, and Ortiz, 1980) document "the shift in commitment to one's ethnic group over time, with a weaker ethnic identity among those who have lived longer in the new country" (Rosenthal and Feldman, 1992). Drawing from other studies (Connor, 1977; Constaninou and Harvey, 1985; Fathi, 1972; Masuda, Hasegawa, and Matsumato, 1973; Masuda, Matsumato, and Meredith, 1970), Rosenthal and Feldman (1992) conclude that "generational differences in ethnic identity tend to show an erosion of ethnic identity in later generations of immigrants" (p. 215). Rosenthal and Feldman (1992) outline in other studies (Wooden, Leon, and Tashima, 1988) that "ethnic identity remains stable after the second generation" and "a resurgence occurs, with stronger identification occurring in third and subsequent generations" (Scourby, 1980; ting-Toomey, 1981). Second-generation Korean-Huaqiaos who have a strong sense of ethnic identity from their first-generation immigrant parents identified themselves fervently along ethnic lines; they preferred Taiwanese education. Current third and fourth-generation Huaqiaos, whose absorption into Korean language and culture is more complete, appear to have a diminished ethnic identity which leads to the shift in college choice among the younger generation Huaqiaos.

The categorizations define the boundaries of particular social groups with which students may identify. Also, ethnic and racial identities are self-defined (Demo and Hughes, 1990), but within the context of the community culture and mainstream culture. In other words, ethnic identity is the degree to which one adopts a social identity based on an ethnic group (Rosenthal and Feldman, 1992).

Based on their research on the visibility of minority students in school, Stanlaw and Peshkin (1988) conclude that ethnic self-identification is complex. Individuals of mixed backgrounds may not want to choose one ethnicity over another, and if they do, they tend to choose the "most ethnic" (p. 215) category. The patriarchal practices of Korean and China, however, do not permit people of mixed parentage to choose their identity: both cultures assign their citizens the ethnicity of their fathers.

Research on Overseas Chinese in Southeast Asia and Chinese Ethnic Identity

Very little research has been done in Korea regarding the Korean-Huaqiaos. Therefore, in this study I will examine studies of Koreans in Japan and also Chinese in Southeast Asian countries as I expect these will provide some evidence against which to compare trends among the Korean-Huaqiaos.

According to a study by Poston, Jr., Mao, and Yu (1994), "almost thirty-seven million overseas Chinese were living in 136 countries [excluding Hong Kong and Macau]" around 1990. Drawing extensively from Wang's (1991) study, the following quote from a study by Poston, Jr., Mao, and Yu (1994, p. 632-633) identifies that there are four major patterns of Chinese migration occurred over the past two centuries.

> The first is the *Huashang* (Chinese trader) pattern, which is characterized by merchants and artisans and, often, their colleagues and members of their extended families, going abroad and eventually setting up business. Often the migrants are males, and over one or two generations many of the unmarried male migrants tend to "settle down and bring up local families" (Wang, 1995: 5). The more their business prospers, the more likely their families are to maintain "their Chinese characteristics, if not all their connections with China" (Wang, 1991: 5). *Huashang* migration has been the dominant pattern in the growth of Chinese emigration to other Asian countries, particularly Southeast Asia before 1850 (Legge, 1886; Yu, 1951; Uchida, 1960; C. P. Fitzgerald, 1965; Yang, 1985). According to Wang the *Huashang* pattern has predominated throughout history. Indeed it is likely that the first recorded Chinese emigration, which was to either Japan, the Philippines, and which occurred during the *Qin* Dynasty (221-207 BC), was the *Huashang* type (Zhu, 1991: 58-59). Whereas the other three patterns have definite temporal periods associated with them, the *Huashang* was and remains the most basic of the Chinese migration patterns (also see Redding, 1990).

Second is the *Huagong* (Chinese coolie) pattern, which occurred from about the 1850s through 1920s, when Chinese migrated to North America and Australia; this migration involved "coolie trade" in gold mining and railway building (Campbell, 1923; McKenzie, 1925; Stewart, 1951; Kung, 1962; Shen, 1970; Zo, 1978; Mei, 1979). Chinese emigrants under the *Huagong* pattern were most often men of peasant origin (Wang, 1991; Wu, 1926). These migrations were in many cases temporary in that a "large proportion of the contract laborers returned to China after their contract came to an end" (Wang, 1991: 6).

Third is the *Huaqiao* (Chinese sojourner) pattern. Although this pattern included all types of migrants, it was strongly comprised of well-educated professionals. This pattern predominated after the fall of imperial China in 1911 and was strongly tied to feelings of nationalism. Education was largely recognized as a deep commitment to promote Chinese culture and national salvation among overseas Chinese. Without Chinese education, there can be no overseas Chinese (S. Fitzgerald, 1972: 41). Beginning in the 1920s, many teachers left China to go abroad to instruct the children of Chinese immigrants in the countries of Southeast Asia (Pan, 1990: 206). This pattern dominated until the 1950s.

The fourth pattern noted by Wang is the *Huayi* (Chinese descent), which he refers to as a more recent phenomenon, prevalent since the 1950s. The pattern involves persons of Chinese descent, *Huayi*, in one foreign country migrating or re-migrating to another foreign country. An example is the Chinese in Southeast Asia who migrated to Western Europe in recent decades, "especially since the 1950s when some Southeast Asian nations made those of Chinese decent feel unwanted" (Wang, 1991: 9).

The study (Poston, Jr., Mao and Yu, 1994) concludes that "Today, the direction and magnitude of Chinese international migration are very much influenced by the migration policies of the sending and receiving countries." Their suggestion that "unless restrictive immigration laws are imposed in all host countries, the growth patterns of the overseas Chinese may tend to be more affected by international emigration and immigration policies than by the demographic processes of fertility and mortality" (p. 643) is pertinent in the Korean setting.

Voluntary migration of the Chinese in Southeast Asia has quite a different outcome than involuntary minorities of different settings. In

John Naisbitt's *Megatrends Asia* (1995), he predicted the ascendance of Asia to global dominance over the coming decades, led by the Overseas Chinese (1995). In *Overseas Chinese Business Networks in Asia* Rees and Sullivan (1995) note that ethnic Chinese often dominate the private, non-land capital of countries where they are a small share of the population. The study attributes their success to thrift, hard work, and an emphasis on education as a portable investment. *The International Economy* (1996) echoes this, and reports that contrary to the popular belief that the Japanese have influenced the East Asian economies, it is actually the Overseas Chinese business community which had the greatest impact on these economies. Further, it asserts that financial markets in China and economic reform in countries such as Thailand, Malaysia, and the Philippines depend on the presence of the Overseas Chinese business community. There has been constant "Suspicion of Chinese settlers in Southeast Asia, even hostility" which brought "occasional massacres of whole communities" (Hicks & Mackie, 1994, July, p. 50).

The Overseas Chinese are the driving energy behind every economy in East Asia, except for Japan and South Korea. Accordingly, three of the four Asian tigers, Hong Kong, Taiwan, and Singapore, have prospered through the efforts of Chinese capitalists, many of whom are now vastly rich. The Fujitsu Research Institute reports remarkable statistics: eighty-one percent of all publicly traded companies in Thailand and Singapore, seventy-three percent in Indonesia, sixty-two percent in Malaysia, and fifty percent in the Philippines are companies in which the majority of ownership is held by people of Chinese extraction (Ziesemer, 1996). In the Philippines, where ethnic Chinese make up just one percent of the population, their companies generate thirty-five percent of the sales of all domestically owned firms. In Indonesia, in the mid 1980s, it was calculated that ethnic Chinese - just over two percent of the population - owned about seventy percent of private domestic capital (*The Economist*, 1993).

The Chinese in Southeast Asia have been subjected to a variety of influences that have led them in different and sometimes conflicting directions. Various other factors such as degrees of acculturation and accommodation of the Chinese to the indigenous culture has influenced the Chinese identity (Gosling, 1983, p. 1). In *Changing Chinese Identities in Southeast Asia: An Introductory Review* Gosling (p. 2) argues that there are four types of adaptation models used by the ethnic Chinese in Southeast Asian countries.

> The earliest and continuing influence is toward adaptation, accommodation, and even assimilation into local societies and cultures. A second shift which has become more powerful in recent decades has

been reemphasis on or in some cases the rise of a common Chinese culture. A third shift has been towards a Western model, first colonial and now a universal modern model. A fourth shift in identity, often prevented or obscured by the previous shifts, is the movement from ethnic identity towards class-based identity.

Lim in her *Chinese Economic Activity in Southeast Asia: An Introductory Review* argues that "In the hierarchical structure of production of developing capitalist economies in Southeast Asia, different levels or stages of economic activity are separated from each other by barriers to entry, in the form of barriers to access to required factors of production" (1983, p. 20). She attributes the clustering of Chinese in urban areas and commerce as following: "In the early stages of development, Chinese immigrants are excluded from peasant production by lack of access to land, and are concentrated in wage labour, while indigenous peasants are excluded from commercial activity by lack of access to capital and market outlets, and are able to avoid wage labour because of their access to land" (p. 20).

Lim notes that in Southeast Asian countries "The state assumes economic importance . . . because it can control access to land, education and wage employment, as it does in Malaysia, using ethnic categories. Ethnic state policies can determine the economic activities not only of the favoured ethnic group, but also of the ethnic groups excluded from access to upward economic mobility" (p. 23). Further, "discrimination against Chinese in education and employment may force them to resort even more to self-employment in order to survive . . . locking them into small- and medium-scale entrepreneurial activities, especially in commerce, and thus, preserving middle-level economic activities" (p. 22).

The Koreans in China, Japan, U.S., and the former Soviet Union

Some minority groups, such as African Americans in the U.S. received intense discrimination and lost much of their cultural heritage while other minority groups have maintained high degrees of cultural autonomy and ethnic identity. Physical and cultural differences between the dominant group and given minority group were used as a tool to explain the pattern of minority group adjustment in the larger society. As such, after comparative examination of the Korean minority in Japan, Min (1992) asserts that "the physical and cultural differences between the majority group and a minority group are not necessary conditions for prejudice and discrimination against ethnic minority group;" rather, "minority groups in different societies make different kinds of adjustment" (p. 4). In *Overseas Koreans and Their Adaptation Patterns*, Choi (1994) concluded that patterns of assimilation, ethnic pluralism, and ethnic conflict are the legacy of history, describing how a given minority group is incorporated into the dominant society, which reflects Ogbu's "cultural ecology" theory of voluntary and involuntary minorities. According to Min (1992), a "high level of ethnic autonomy and positive ethnic identify of Koreans in China are the result of a 'pluralistic minority policy emphasizing ethnic autonomy'" (p. 4-21). The Koreans in China enjoy a high degree of economic and educational success higher than that of *Han* majority. On the other hand, Koreans in Japan present a contrary picture. Although the period of migration was approximately the same period, Koreans in Japan are an involuntary minority, comprised mostly of forced laborers and military conscripts under the colonial rule. This "historical legacy of Japanese imperialism" (Lie, 1987) still persists, and the Koreans in Japan are subject to institutional and personal discrimination under the Japanese government's "monolithic assimilationist policy" (Min, 1992). As a result, the Koreans in Japan "lost much of their cultural repertoire and suffered from negative ethnic identity" (Min 1992, p. 19). As Rohlen (1981, p. 199) notes, Koreans in Japan are "Children without a tomorrow"; sports and entertainment are the only way to social mobility (Lie, 1987). The experience of Koreans in Japan as an involuntary minority parallels the experiences of the involuntary minority of African Americans and Hispanic-Americans in the United States whose discrimination has been both institutional as well as personal thus in compliance with Ogbu's "cultural ecology" theory.

Research on Citizenship/National Policy/Geopolitics

Marshall notes that "Citizenship is a status bestowed on those who are full members of a community. . . All who possess the status are equal with respect to the rights and duties with which the status is endowed" (Marshall and Bottomore, 1992, p. 18). For Marshall "the right of the citizen . . . is the right to equality of opportunity" (p. 65), and further, the "equality of status is more important than equality of income" (p. 56). According to Marshall (1950; 1992) citizenship consists of three elements: civil, political, and social. The civil element is "composed of the rights necessary for individual freedom - liberty of the person, freedom of speech, thought and faith, the right to own property and to conclude valid contracts, and the right to justice" (Marshall, 1950; Marshall and Bottomore, 1992, p. 8). Marshall (1950; 1992) maintains that the right to justice is "the right to defend and assert all one's rights on terms of equality with others and by due process of law" through the courts of justice. The political element of citizenship is "to participate in the exercise of political power, as a member of a body invested with political authority or as an elector of the members of such a body," such as parliament and councils of local government. On the other hand, the social element "range[s] from the right to a modicum of economic welfare and security to the right to share to the full in the social heritage and to live the life of a civilised being according to the standards prevailing in the society. [Therefore, by definition] The institutions most closely connected with it are the educational system and the social service" (Marshall and Bottomore, 1992, p. 8). Noting that "Citizenship defines the relationship between individuals and the state," Klausen (1995, p. 249) drawing from Rogers Brubaker (1995, p. 249) asserted that "the process of state building affects the norms of citizenship" (Hobsbawm, 1993 in Klausen, 1995, p. 249). For example, a person who was born in 1917 and lived "in certain areas of Eastern Europe may have changed citizenship four or five times without ever having moved" (Hobsbawm, 1993 in Klausen, 1995, p. 249). As such, national boundaries and citizenship are altering as political changes are taking place. National boundaries and citizenship are, therefore, subject to political changes. However, scholarly discussion on citizenship rights is often limited to citizens; leaving the rights of non-citizens still ambiguous and a point of controversy in most countries.

In discussing the requirement for citizenship, Gallstone, (1993 in Klausen, 1995, p. 249) noted that "sense of the community" and "loyalty" are associated with "communitarian views of rights and obligation in the democratic state," thus his suggest that "belonging requires the consent of the community" (Klausen, 1995, p. 250). Elaborating on Gallstone's view, Klausen (1995) contends that the modern "welfare state has in effect intensified the importance of belonging to these communities" as a result of the elevated level of the state's obligation toward its citizens. As Korea becomes a more industrialized nation, the issue of citizenship becomes more complex than before and is expected to become controversial.

As was established in the Korean nationality law section of this study, Huaqiaos are precluded from Korean nationality through citizenship law which emphasizes an individual's "blood," specifically partrilineal blood. Such a nationality law is not pragmatic when considering that a person with a Korean father is entitled to Korean citizenship, even though this person may never have been in Korea, and, at the same time, foreign residents, who have lived in Korea for generations, are still considered foreign nationals. Such impracticality is exemplified in those children of mixed unions, when Korean nationality law keeps them in a state of limbo, especially the children of Korean mothers and Huaqiao fathers. While these children culturally, linguistically, and biologically identify themselves as Koreans, legally they are a foreign population. Legal preclusion from Korean citizenship appears to induce Korean-Huaqiaos to associate closer to their Chinese identity. Stalaw and Peshkin's (1988) findings support the fact that people with mixed backgrounds tend to choose the "most ethnic" identity when they must. These finding coincide with Gosling's (1983) findings in a study of Chinese in Southeast Asian countries regarding how government policy affects Chinese identity. The unequal citizenship status of Korean-Huaqiaos appears to be a source of Huaqiaos' reluctance to more closely identify themselves with Korea.

Vermelen and Pels (1984) state that one dimension of ethnicity is "historical." According to them, the historical dimension "offers interpretations of the past." At the same time, it provides "an 'answer' to a specific situation [which] can be only understood as being influenced by historical experience" (p. 281). This study challenges Ogbu's definition of "voluntary minority" and "involuntary minority" status and suggests that such statuses are flexible according to political change. On the other hand, it is closely aligned to the view of Nagel (1994, p. 152) who asserted that "the construction of ethnic identity and culture is the result of both structure and agency - a dialectic played out by ethnic groups and the larger society."

Research on the Influence of Market Pressures and Rewards

In *The Chinese in Southeast Asia*, Gosling (1983, p. 1) observes that "ethnic identity would be weakened as national capitalist economic development (as opposed to colonial capitalist economic development) preceded, and that class identity and divisions would replace ethnic identity and divisions." In a similar manner, Sow's (1983) study of the Chinese in Malaysia reports that an increasing number of Chinese are converted to Islam in the desire to gain "membership in the national culture," which will also bring material reward. In discussing what Hechter (1984) terms as a "cultural division of labor," Vermeulen and Pels assert that "concentration of an ethnic group in specific class or socio-economic stratum or in a particular occupation or cluster of occupations may provide a basis for intra-ethnic interaction and common interests and may influence the opinions and attitudes of outsiders toward the group's self-image" (p. 279).

Chapter Three
Methodology

This chapter will present the information-gathering methods in an attempt to answer the overarching question and the sub-questions presented in Chapter One.

The aim of this study was to find out "why" there has been a shift in the earlier demand for Taiwanese universities to Korean universities. The major data was derived from the perceptions of students, teachers, parents, community leaders, and alumni through in-depth interviews. Data was gathered in a quantitative survey first. The data was then used for the qualitative study done in the interviews. In addition to the interviews and a survey, other information was obtained from internal school documents of the Seoul Overseas Chinese High School and the Seoul Overseas Elementary School.

This chapter will first describe the purpose of the study, the rationale of the qualitative approach used, the population and the sample, the development of the instruments, and the methods of data analysis.

Purpose of the Study

The purpose of this study was to discover the underlying social and policy elements behind the change in ethnic Chinese students' choices in higher education. The following sub-questions were asked, to answer the main research questions:

1. What quantitative shift occurred that led Chinese students in Korea to select Korean universities over Taiwanese universities?
2. What were the Korean government's and the Taiwanese government's recent social, economic, and educational policies

toward the ethnic Chinese in Korea, and how did these policies influence the educational choices of the ethnic Chinese?

3.   What are the advantages and disadvantages of studying in Korean universities versus Taiwanese universities? (Did the Chinese students who chose the Korean university consider the Taiwanese universities and vice-versa, and how seriously did they consider other options?; Why do Chinese students choose one track as opposed to the other?; Why do Chinese students choose to go to Korean/Taiwanese universities?)

4.   What do students, parents, teachers, and community leaders think has changed so that students now predominantly choose Korean universities rather than Taiwanese universities?

5.   How does community choice influence individual choice?

Case Study

Hammersley (1992) defines the case study as "the phenomenon (located in space/time) about which data are collected and/or analyzed, and that corresponds to the type of phenomena to which the main claims of a study relate" (p. 184). The case study affords the researcher greater detail, a higher likelihood of accuracy, all of which are important to the collection of data sufficient to answer the research questions. According to Yin (1984), "the case study's unique strength is its ability to deal with a full variety of evidence-document, artifacts, interviews, and observations" (p20).

Bromley (1986) writes that case studies, by definition, "get as close to the subject of interest as they possibly can, partly by means of direct observation in natural settings, partly by their access to subjective factors (thoughts, feelings, and desires), whereas experiments and surveys often use convenient derivative data such as test results, official records (p. 23)." Also case studies tend to spread the net for evidence widely, whereas experiments and survey usually have a narrow focus. The case study does not claim any particular methods for data collection (Merriam, 1988)

Qualitative Approach

A qualitative research design was used in this study. A growing number of researchers suggest the need for qualitative studies which will take into account the context-laden nature of topics of interest (Miles and Huberman, 1984; Firestone, 1993; Teddlie and Stringfield, 1993). Many scholars in the field of education urge insights into process rather than outcomes, into context rather than specific variables, into discovery rather than confirmation (Merriam, 1988).

For Levin and Lezotte (1990), some of the most useful knowledge concerning school [institutional] effects has been produced in case studies of schools that allow for an in-depth understanding of the situation and its meaning for those involved. Merriam (1988) believes that research focused on discovery, insight, and understanding from the perspective of those being studied offers the greatest promise of making significant contributions to the knowledge base and practice of education. Lincoln (1990) has characterized inquiry as done in natural contexts where realities were captured holistically. How people make sense of their lives, what they experience, how they interpret these experiences, how they structure their social world is keen of interest to qualitative researchers (Merriam, 1988). Many researchers consider the case study as the most suitable research strategy to effect such types of inquiry (Merriam, 1988; Hammersley, 1992; Yin, 1994).

Interview

The qualitative methodology of the semi-structured interview was employed. The purpose of the interviews was to acquire an understanding of the relationship between the social milieu and the ethnic Chinese in Korea. Interviews of five community leaders, twelve students, five teachers, four parents, five alumni were conducted during the month of August 1998. I asked students questions regarding their future aspirations, such as their career expectations, their methods of achieving these goals, and how Korean universities fit these expectations. Out of the respondents to questionnaires, twelve interviewees were chosen on a volunteer basis: four males and eight females, representing both high and low levels of academic standing. Other individuals, such as alumni and community leaders, were chosen with the assistance of teachers. Parents were selected on a volunteer basis among the respondents to questionnaires. Some of the interviews were by telephone due to the time constraints of interviewees.

Interview Protocol

Eisner (1981) considers qualitative research with the interview process as an art form where the researcher reflects the study with a binocular vision that has depth of field. In this method the researcher can make generalizations of a particular nature in order to be informative. The researcher will thereby obtain data through interaction with participants. Borg and Gall (1993) supported the purpose of a qualitative interview as aiming to develop an understanding of the perceptions of participants. Cadewell and Hill (1988) supported the interview process as a way of developing a rapport between the interviewer and interviewees. Rubin and Rubin (1995) have defined the qualitative interviewing strategy as "guided conversations," and have suggested interviewing should be conducted as an ordinary conversation. At the same time, this strategy requires the interviewer to listen carefully to the meaning of what is being said, and then ask the right questions with the proper wording. Conversations will focus on a narrow range of topics in order to obtain more in-depth and detailed information. "In interviews, the researcher gently guides the discussion, leading it through stages, asking specific questions, and encouraging the interviewee to answer in depth and at length" (Rubin and Rubin, 1995, p. 124).

In this study, a set of primary questions was prepared before each interview. In order to obtain the maximum amount of information, the purpose of the study was briefly summarized at the beginning of the interview.

Document Analysis

Document analysis was employed "to corroborate and augment evidence from other sources" (Yin, 1994, p. 81). Lasswell (1968) argues that comparison "is so central to good analysis that scientific method is unavoidably comparative" (cited in Collier, 1991, p.7). Studies of Southeast Asian countries regarding Huaqiaos were examined to provide a sense of perspective.

According to Wang (1981), there are two different ways the word "history" may be used. Both refer to the past, but one describes our knowledge or perception of the past and the other relates to the actions and developments that have already taken place in the past.

In this study, I have primarily dealt with the former concept of "history" since many of the elements which influenced the development of the ethnic Chinese community in Korea will be revealed through what is knowable, in the form of documents, records, oral documents and other artifacts as a mode of knowledge. Available internal school documents and other data, such as population and government policies, that were thought to have influenced the educational choices of the Korean-Huaqiaos, were examined.

Background information was drawn from the analysis of internal and external documents of the Seoul Overseas Chinese High School through examination of the shift in trends and changes in curriculum that have been made to meet new demands. Other sources, such as newspapers, magazines, personal letters, records from the Taipei

Mission (Taiwanese Council), and the documents from the Overseas Chinese Association in Korea, were utilized to look into demographic information.

The process of compiling the documents and analyzing them was the first step taken. This analysis provided important background information on the past and current situation, especially recent trends in schooling among the Chinese in Korea. Also, it indicated the way in which the educational policies of South Korean and Taiwanese governments have had an impact on the ethnic Chinese in Korea. The information obtained will provide insight into the relevant areas that will be probed in greater depth by interviews. It will also be useful in better understanding the responses to the questionnaires, and this will provide the necessary perspective to get answers to research questions.

Data will be collected for a period of at least 10 years to calculate both the percentage of Chinese in Korea at Taiwanese universities and the percentage of Chinese students in Korean universities. The results are presented in graphical forms and tables. This documented evidence served as an introduction to the main question of this case study: what educational choice is being pursued by young Chinese in Korea and why; what cultural and economic trend does it reflect?

Quantitative Approach

A survey instrument was also used in this study. The purpose of administering questionnaires was to reach a broader spectrum of the Huaqiao High School student population whom the researcher would otherwise be unable to reach through the in-depth interviews, due to time constraints.

Schuman (1981) claimed that polls and surveys are an extremely efficient method of obtaining information. When the speed of computer processing and the power of multivariate analysis are added to the more basic ingredients of questions and samples, the whole can yield information and insights about a large population that would be impossible to obtain in any other way. The foremost advantage of the sample survey technique ". . . is the ability to generalize about an entire population by drawing inferences based on data drawn from a small portion of that population" (Parker, 1997). While the cost of conducting a sample survey is significantly less than that of canvassing the entire population and can be implemented in a timely fashion, ". . . the sample survey is a reasonably accurate method of collecting data. It offers an opportunity to reveal the characteristics of institutions and communities by studying individuals who represent these entities in a relatively unbiased and scientifically rigorous manner" (Parker, 1997). Further,

Parker claimed that the survey offers the advantage of a "snapshot" of a population. It also offers the advantage of replicability. A questionnaire used by Dixon and Martin (1991) was modified and expanded and then administered to the entire class of Korean University Track students and the Taiwanese University Track students to explore the factors influencing choices of higher education among the ethnic Chinese in Korea. The students were asked to make subjective judgments in responding to the questions, using a six-degree Likert-scale. While some questions were direct and factual, others dealt more with a student's personal perception and required interpretation on the part of the researcher. A questionnaire containing 121 items, pertaining to five categories, was collected from 134 senior students of the Seoul Overseas Chinese High School. The students took the survey home and student representatives from each class collected the survey for this researcher.

Pilot Study

The pilot study was conducted in Seoul Overseas High School with a sample size of twelve senior students, which was balanced for gender and track. Eight students from the Korean university track and four students from the Taiwanese university track: five females and three males from the Korean university track, and two males and two females from the Taiwanese university track responded to test the reliability of the study. The survey data from the pilot study was not used in this study. However, the interviews have been incorporated.

Methods of Analysis

Miles and Huberman (1984) indicate the importance of displays in data analysis. The survey data was coded in spss and mean-score, frequency, T-table and/or ANOVA for each factor was computed and described.

   With the interviewees' permission, the interviews were tape recorded and transcribed. For interviews with those who declined the tape recording request, I wrote a summary post-actively. I made it clear that participation was voluntary, and that the interviewees could decline the interview at anytime during the process. They were assured of their anonymity.

Validity and Reliability

Merriam (1988) noted that internal validity, reliability, and external validity are criteria by which to judge research and its outcome.

Internal Validity

Merriam (1988) asserts that internal validity assesses how well the researcher captures the subjects' constructions of reality. "Validity must be assessed in terms of interpreting the investigator's experience, rather than in terms of reality itself (which can never be grasped)" (Merriam, 1988, p. 167). Triangulation is an important strategy to provide evidence of validity.

Triangulation

Triangulation involves "using multiple investigators, multiple sources of data, or multiple methods to confirm the emerging findings" (Merriam, 1988, p. 169). The document analysis, the survey, and the interview provided an opportunity for triangulation. Triangulation allows the possibility to look into "what," "why," and "how." Commonalties and differences by track, gender, academic preparedness and the type of respondents were considered. The emphasis was on looking into causes and effects of policies that influence educational choices by Korean-Huaqiaos.

Reliability

Citing Lincoln and Guba (1995), Merriam (1988) concurs that reliability in a qualitative case study demands that "given the data collected, the results make sense — they are consistent and dependable"(p. 172). The main strategy used to provide evidence of reliability in this research is triangulation that strengthens claims of reliability as well as internal validity.

External Validity

Merriam (1988) suggests that "reader or user generalizability [is] particularly suited to case study research" (p. 176-177). External validity then rests with the reader's assessment of the believability of the results and their usefulness to the reader. Such an assessment depends on the researcher's ability to provide a description of the case that is sufficient to furnish the reader with the ability to assess the utility of the conclusions.

Yin (1984) provides an additional measure for assessment of external validity, that of "analytical generalization [in which] the investigator is striving to generalize a particular set of results to some broader theory" (p. 36).

Ethical Considerations

I obtained permission to do this research through telephone conversations with the Seoul Overseas Chinese High School principal who was my math teacher during my high school career. Due to the cultural context in which a verbal agreement is valid, I did not request written permission. I was allowed to make use of the homeroom period to distribute the surveys to the students. The students were allowed to take the survey home. On the survey form I attached an explanation of the purpose of the study and the fact that participation was voluntary. I clarified that the purpose of this research was singularly academic and not that it was intended to investigate a private citizen or to benefit any specific organization. Confidentiality was assured. Also, I requested the signed consent of the parents if/when a student was willing to participate. One hundred thirty-four students out of 170 students participated in the survey. Willing parents were selected for interviews from the survey. The interviews with the teachers, students, and the principal took place at the school, while alumni and community leaders were interviewed in various places to accommodate needs of the interviewees.

Limitations of the Study

This study is limited to an examination of educational issues and behavior among the ethnic Chinese in Korea. It will be difficult to depend thoroughly on scientific theory or measurement in order to answer the questions in this research. The availability of data, such as the school records, was expected to be a problem for collection in this research. As an alumna of SOCHS I had easy access to this population group, and my background may have led them to open up to me more easily, thus providing in-depth knowledge. Recognizing that interpretation and judgment inevitably involve some degree of subjectivity, my perspective as a Korean and a person who has lived abroad in the American and other pluralist societies, however, may have provided the necessary objectivity for this research.

Conclusions

I expect this study to provide an understanding of economic, cultural, social, and domestic as well as international political factors influencing educational choice among young ethnic Chinese in Korea. This is a very homogeneous and small minority whose behavior may illuminate social policies and educational issues among other small minority communities elsewhere.

Chapter Four

Definition of Overseas-Chinese, The Korean Nationality Law and the Demography of the Korean-Chinese

This chapter provides a brief definition of the term "Overseas-Chinese," of which the Korean-Chinese are a sub-group, followed by an overview of the demographic background of the ethnic Chinese in Korea, and a summary of their social and educational history in the context of Korean society.

Definition of Overseas-Chinese and Korean-Chinese

In his book, *The Future of the Overseas Chinese in Southeast Asia*, Lea Williams defines "Overseas Chinese" as follows:

> an overseas Chinese is a person of some Chinese ancestry who views residence abroad as compatible with Chinese cultural identity and less certainly with some remote Chinese political orientation. The overseas Chinese considers his expatriation the result of his own or his forebears' economic strivings. He regards himself as a member of the overseas Chinese people, which is in turn, part of the greater Chinese nation, and is so regarded by those around him (p. 6).

Williams observes that the Overseas-Chinese are similar to either the *"pieds noirs* of Algeria, who claimed French identity although they were often generations removed from Europe, or to those New Zealanders who an occasion speak of England as home" (p. 6).

> The Chinese overseas have been regarded by recent Chinese governments as the full members of China's political family. Until a

short time ago the expatriates and all their descendants through
the male line over infinite generations were officially classified as
citizens of China. Every Chinese census or attempt at population
count tallied the Chinese abroad as well as those within the state
frontiers of China. Such official attachment to *jus sanguinis* was
merely formal recognition of the force of the feeling of the overseas
Chinese that together with Chinese in China they were *t'ung-pao*,
children of the same womb (p. 4).

Noting that "No definition can be unfailingly sharp and concise
because the decision on whether or not a man or a group is overseas
Chinese is made by governments, both Chinese and foreign, by the larger societies alongside and within which Chinese settlers live, and the
innumerable individuals" (p. 5), Williams asserts that overseas Chinese
identity is based more on personal social attitudes than official legislation. He further elaborates that "Chinese ancestry, at least on the
father's side, is clearly essential." But "Births in China is by no means
a basic requirement" as "today most overseas Chinese were born far
from their ancestral villages. Foreign residence must be extended or
permanent. A Chinese student, diplomat, or merchant away from
China for a specific purpose and definite period is not an overseas
Chinese" (p. 5).

The difficulty of determining a man's membership in the overseas
Chinese is compounded by the fact that individual attitudes are of
central relevance. A person who considers himself overseas Chinese
and is accepted as such by the Chinese and non-Chinese in his area
clearly qualifies. More troublesome is the person who lives in sprit
between the overseas Chinese and the indigenous populations.
Many persons of Chinese ancestry are now in a transitional state
between overseas Chinese identity and assimilation. There are
those who rarely think of their Chinese ancestry, and are not now
overseas Chinese but who could be pushed into active Chinese identification by the refusal of the governments and the indigenous peo-
ples of their overseas homelands to permit the absorption of ethnic
Chinese into the nation. On the reverse side of this slippery coin,
men who now have only limited awareness of overseas Chinese connections could be drawn toward final assimilation with the historical precedent. In the past, some Chinese have disappeared into the
Southeast Asian masses, while others have been pushed back from
the brink of assimilation (p. 6).

Therefore, although "The English term *overseas Chinese* is general and familiar" it is not clear and "rests on too many intangibles" while the Chinese term Huaqiao, meaning Chinese sojourning abroad, offers a bit more precise definition. To a Chinese speaker, Huaqiao "are expatriates linked at least in a vague emotional way to China and in a more discernable manner to Chinese culture" (p. 6).

A definition of Korean- Huaqiao is less ambiguous as most Korean-Huaqiaos have not attained Korean citizenship but are citizens of Taiwan, and they have a strong political and educational affiliation with that country. They usually consider themselves to be returning to their motherland when they go to Taiwan. At the same time the majority of Korean- Huaqiaos remain emotionally attached to China. Since both Korean and Chinese convention mark the place of residence as a modifier before the country of citizenship/ethnic designation, I will use the term Korean- Huaqiao(s) and Korean-Chinese interchangeably.

Immigration, Naturalization and Citizenship Policies

Korean nationality laws, which imply that there are distinctions between the citizen and non-citizen, and accordingly, between their respective rights and duties, have affected the Korean-Huaqiaos' educational choices, their participation in politics, and their economic well-being. As non-citizens, male Korean-Huaqiaos are exempted from compulsory military service, which their Korean male counterparts must fulfill, and they have greater choice in education as they are not required by Korean educational law to send their children to Korean schools. On the other hand, they are prohibited from political participation, and they contend that they have limited economic and occupational mobility. Many Huaqiaos whom I interviewed expressed their opinion that the Korean naturalization law is unfriendly and designed for selective naturalization "for those who are wealthy and have connections in the [Korean] government," while Koreans believe Korean-Huaqiaos lack an earnest desire to become Korean.

The first requirement for any kind of citizenship is belonging to the state community. Historically and conceptually, citizenship has always implied the exclusion of those who do not belong to the protective community. Originally denoting residence within the protective walls of cities, citizenship defines a community by establishing who may reside within the boundaries and who may not. Borders are changeable, as are the definitions and standards of citizenship. Wars, migration, and annexations are important causes of change (Hobsbawm, 1993). Hobsbawm has estimated that a person born in certain areas of

Eastern Europe in 1917 might have changed citizenship four or five times without ever having moved as a result of shifting borders. Therefore, the process of state building affects the norms of citizenship and also its relationship with non-citizens.

The Korean nationality law of 1948 dictated two ways to obtain Korean nationality: first, through birth by Korean parent(s), and, second, through naturalization. Korean law does not acknowledge dual citizenship even now. Until its modification in 1998, partrilineal Korean law granted Korean nationality to those who were born to Korean fathers regardless of the place of birth. According to this law, if the father was a foreign national and the mother was Korean, then the child was not entitled to Korean nationality by birth even though he/she was born in Korea, and if a child of such a union wished to choose Korean nationality, he or she had to apply to the Minister of Justice for permission for naturalization. Therefore, children of marriages between Huaqiao men and Korean women were unable to acquire Korean citizenship by birth unless the Chinese fathers were naturalized prior to the birth of their children. On the other hand, Huaqiao women who were married to Korean men automatically became Korean nationals. When a foreign national male married a Korean female, he could maintain his previous nationality. If he wished to become naturalized, he had to reside in Korea for three years and obtain permission from the Minister of Justice. However, when a foreign female married a Korean male, she automatically became Korean whether she wanted to or not. Similarly, when a foreign male became naturalized, his wife also became a Korean national regardless of her wishes. A married foreign female (to a foreign male), however, could only become naturalized when accompanied by her husband. This law was essentially compatible with the laws of Taiwan and mainland China, as noted earlier.

As of June 1998, a person with a Korean parent, regardless of the other parent's citizenship, may obtain Korean citizenship by birth. Other legal changes were also made. In the past, if a Korean male adopted a child, he/she automatically became a Korean national. However, the new law dictates that one must obtain permission to apply for citizenship from the Minister of Justice. According to the new law, both the male and the female must reside in Korea for two years in order to become naturalized by marriage. This law is designed to prohibit bogus marriages in an effort to obtain Korean nationality. The new law also abolished the clause that required the husband to accompany his wife if she desired to become a Korean national. Also, a foreign national woman does not automatically become a Korean national when she marries a Korean man. She also must apply for naturalization. It is too early for any study to gauge the impact of the revision, and, since the present study was conducted in the summer of 1998, the data discussed here reflect the influence of the old laws.

The Korean naturalization law declares that a person who wishes to become naturalized must have assets of 4,000,000 won (equivalent to approximately 40,000 US dollars) and be sponsored by two high-ranking government officers. In addition, a candidate must convince the naturalization authority that he/she is a contributing member of Korean society. Not surprisingly, many Huaqiaos feel that the Korean laws are designed to keep poor Huaqiaos as foreign nationals:

> There are certain practical benefits of being naturalized if one lives in Korea. But with such outrageous requirements how can many of us become naturalized? If such a law were applied to Koreans, there wouldn't be many Koreans.

Another interviewee feels:

> The Korean government doesn't want poor Huaqiaos. Only wealthy Huaqiaos with a connection in the government can become naturalized.

Naturally, there is hint of envy towards those who became naturalized Korean citizens while others remain skeptical about the prospect of being able to do so. The following story is widely known among the Huaqiaos and there are a few similar cases, which further convince the Huaqiao community that the naturalization law in Korea is very discriminatory. Mr. L was a third generation Huaqiao, and was employed as a Korean bank clerk upon graduation from a Korean university. Opportunities for employment in Korean companies are hard to come by and, naturally, Mr. L was very happy to have a job and he worked extra hard to succeed. He also showed exceptional talent in banking and drew the most customers and the largest deposits. The bank awarded Mr. L several times for his extraordinary work. Naturally, Mr. L envisioned becoming a chief executive manager of the bank some day. He knew that Korean citizenship was essential to achieve this, so he applied for naturalization. To his dismay, his petition was denied on the ground that there was no evidence that he was a contributing member to Korea. He reapplied, only to be denied again. The clause "contributing member to Korean society" left the bureaucracy much leeway to make a subjective judgment. In the meantime Mr. L wasn't even considered for a promotion, while his less able peers moved up. Frustrated, Mr. L finally quit his job and emigrated to the United States. In the absence of clear-cut guidelines in policies, ambiguities in interpretation and bureaucratic red tape are the government's safest way out.

Koreans and Huaqiaos differ in interpretation of the naturalization law. With regards to requiring four million won in assets as a condition for naturalization, one Korean law professor explains:

> It is not a big deal. Practically anyone who has a house has that much in assets, and most people own a house. Besides, there are agencies which will help with all the necessary paperwork, including finding the sponsors and temporarily transferring money to a bank account for a small fee.

The temporary electronic transfer of money to a bank account is a popular practice in Korea when there is a requirement for proof of some kind of assets. As a common practice, a new employee is often requested to provide "proof of assets" in order to guarantee the employee's reliability. Those who do not have such assets must have someone vouch for them. There are many cases where such "good will" does not work out. In such cases, sureties bear the burden of the sponsored individual's misfortune or wrongdoings. The electronic transfer of money is popular as it frees both the render and the receiver of any burden. Recently, with overseas travel becoming popular, the need for a "financial voucher" has become even more prevalent. Because the electronic transfer of money has become such a popular practice, many Koreans as well as Huaqiaos utilize this system. Thus, some Koreans are convinced that the Huaqiaos' allegation of tough naturalization laws as an obstacle to citizenship is rather flimsy. While Koreans in general are convinced that the Huaqiaos display a rather passionate ethnic identity that prevents them from being naturalized, both groups recognize the need for some kind of provisions to secure the legal status of the Huaqiaos on humanitarian grounds.

Korea does not have a legal provision for permanent resident aliens. Therefore, even though most Chinese-Koreans are born and educated in South Korea, they are treated like ordinary foreigners and are required to renew their resident visas every three years. Until lately, the reentry visa was limited to a single, one-year entry. This law caused much inconvenience to many Huaqiaos and their families. According to an interviewee:

> When I was studying in Taiwan, something happened and I wasn't able to return to Korea within the permitted time [one year]. When my visa expired, the Korean government refused to renew it. My parents and siblings were in Korea, but I was not allowed to return. I petitioned various government offices but in vain. They tossed me between the Ministry of Foreign Affairs and the Ministry of Justice. The Ministry of Foreign Affairs insisted that I have my visa

renewed, while the Ministry of Justice conceded that it was not required, as I am a permanent resident alien. I was only able to return to Korea and meet my parents after I became a Taiwanese diplomat.

Similar stories were related by other interviewees. Mrs. Z was visiting her son, who was studying at a Taiwanese university. Toward the end of her visit, she was hospitalized with appendicitis. While she was in the hospital, her visa expired and her request to renew it was denied. The family petitioned the Korean government but it was no use. A few years later, Mr. Z finally sold his restaurant in Korea and moved to Taiwan to reunite with his wife. This law had been modified in 1996 when the renewal period was extended to five years and the visa also extended to two-year multiple entries. Although belatedly, this provision was made for those whose residency statuses were revoked prior to the change in law.

The younger generation Huaqiaos, who are very vocal, question the civility of these laws that bind them as foreign nationals to the only country they know. They assert that they should be given at least a choice of whether to be Taiwanese or to become a Korean national upon legal age, without going through the naturalization process. An interviewee who now works at the Taipei Mission declares:

> I am a second-generation Huaqiao. My father came alone to Korea when he was about seventeen. It was prior to the Korean War. We are often called Huaqiao but it is incorrect. We are second-generation Huaqiaos. For example, let's talk about Koreans. Koreans who emigrated to the United States are given to resident alien status [by the United States government]. They can live in the United States as long as they wish. When they reside in the United States for five years, they are given the right to apply for citizenship. The children of these people are United States citizens with Korean ancestry. They are not Korean citizens. The Korean government refers to them as second-generation Korean émigrés. On the other hand, I was born in Korea. Am I a Huaqiao or a Korean citizen? This is a very critical point. I was born in Korea, and I have a right and duty to be a Korean [but I am not].

The following story that is well known among the Huaqiao community illuminates the paradox of the Korean nationality law. Ms. A is a Korean woman. She married a Huaqiao man and was naturalized as a Taiwanese national, as custom dictated at the time. Her husband died soon after they had a daughter. With her husband gone, she had no relation or friend in the Huaqiao community. She sent her daughter to

Korean schools. Upon graduation from high school, Mrs. A and her daughter realized that it was practically impossible for her as a Huaqiao to get a job. So, they sustained their living by earning money as street vendors. For any legal matters she has to go to the Huaqiao community, which is virtually foreign to her. When they had saved enough money to buy a house, the mother and daughter learned that as foreign nationals they could not own a house. The situation regarding the ownership of property by foreign nationals has improved, but the Huaqiao community believes these laws are manifestations of Korean exclusiveness. Many Koreans agree that provisions such as that of permanent alien"in the United States, must be made for those aliens who have been living in Korea for a long period of time, such as the Huaqiaos.

As foreign nationals, Huaqiaos cannot engage in Korean politics. In addition to being a small population, the Huaqiaos are vulnerable to policy changes as they have no representation in the Korean political system. Professor J of Seoul National University, feels sympathetic to the Huaqiaos' plight, and asserts that "some improvements have been made but much more needs to be done in regard to the Huaqiao situation in Korea." But, he adds, "Huaqiaos themselves only complain. No actual work is done. They seem unable to do anything for their own cause." Prof. J related a personal experience in working with the Huaqiaos. As part of a graduate project, he investigated the legal position of this population group. Startled to find out about the Huaqiaos' plight, and sympathetic to them, he invited the news media to talk about Huaqiao causes and requested support from the Huaqiao community in doing this.

> They were all eager at first. But somehow they changed their mind and, further, they reported my activities to the police. I was questioned by the police for my activities. They were not only unable to work for their own cause but were also not so helpful to those championing their cause.

Professor J estimated that Huaqiao reluctance was from the fear of the possibility of the Korean government's harassment if they spoke ill about its policy. He thinks that such a passive approach by the Huaqiao community did not help their progress in Korean society. Some younger generation Huaqiao understand Professor J's point. They feel that their community needs to evaluate itself before blindly criticizing the Korean government for discrimination.

> We [Huaqiaos] must bear partial responsibility for what is happening in Korea. Our forefathers neglected to educate the younger generation of Huaqiaos to assimilate to Korean society; instead

they perpetuated their old [Chinese] ways in Korea. Even in China things have changed, and some of the old ways are no longer useful. In this way, our failure in Korea is rather inevitable. It is logical for any country to put the interest of their citizens first. Our forefathers had a mentality of sojourners. As sojourners they expected Korean society to cater to their wants and needs. Everything has to be reciprocal. If we are going to live in Korea then we have to do our part. Assimilating into Korean society is natural and should be recommended. Naturalization is one way. Fortunately, an increasing number of younger generations have become naturalized. I think it is good. We are living in Korea and must adapt to Korea. Older generation Huaqiaos don't want to hear about it, but things are changing.

Recently, increasing numbers of Huaqiaos have become naturalized. Mr. C is one of those few. His wife is Korean, and he sent his son to a nearby Korean school. He explains his experience:

I studied Political Science and learned about political theories. And I have come to think that national borders or citizenship are not of fundamental importance to men. The more direct reason is that I have studied seven years in Taiwan. During that time I worked about two years at the Central Research Institute. I was having financial difficulty — I was married and accompanied by my wife and had to support my new family. I tried many places to look for work. There was a magazine called *Korean-China Culture* that was published in Korea at that time. I worked as a reporter for three years. There was another gentleman named Mr. Wang. Along with him we had to do everything by ourselves. It was lots of work and very difficult. I liked to write, and I saw an advertisement for a daily news reporter by a Taiwanese newspaper. I wanted to apply. In the application there was a section asking for my membership number to the KMT (Nationalist Party) along with other information. I was shocked to find that reporters were required membership in the KMT. I am not a KMT member and thought that I had very slim chance of obtaining the position. As I suspected, I was not selected for the job. After that experience I applied many places, and finally found a job in the private sector. It was a temporary job [until I finished my school]. I didn't have any relatives or alumni connections [to speak of] in Taiwan. So I decided to take a *Kuoko*, the civil service exams for government administration and for the Foreign Service. On one occasion, the exam was given to select three Foreign Service officers. I had prepared well in all subjects, and I chose Korean as a foreign language. I knew I would do well. About fourty people applied and I was fourth. The administrator's exam was the same. On all my other exams, I always ended up right below the cut-off line. I asked my friends who were my classmates at the School of Political Science graduate school of Taiwan National University, who were in high positions such as secretary of the Generalisimo's Office, administrator of the State Office, etc. for an explanation. After talking with them, I came to the conclusion that there is friction between the Taiwanese and the mainland groups. Even the mainland group was fractionalized within itself on account of individuals' places of origin, i.e. Kwangdong, Shansi, and Beijing, etc. The Taiwanese make arrangements to balance these factions. Overseas-Chinese are at the bottom of the list after all these factions are arranged. Therefore, the Overseas-Chinese are outsiders. We are neither Taiwanese nor mainlanders. No one to champion our interests. So, I decided to return to Korea. I didn't belong there [Taiwan].

Mr. C's statement is significant in understanding the status of the Huaqiaos' in terms of the Taiwanese political reality. Under such circumstances, the Korean-Huaqiaos have begun to realize that they are outsiders in both societies, and thus have started to seek to improve their lot in their adopted country — Korea. In order to live in Korea, Korean-Huaqiaos agree that "studying in Korean universities is infinitely more advantageous."

Mr. C thinks he represents a successful example of adaptation to Korea, and he adds that the timing was good also.

During the 1980s there was a great expansion of Chinese studies—language and literature—at Korean universities. I taught during the day while I was studying in a doctoral program.

The final reason he chose naturalization was:

Although my Korean colleagues were very cordial, I felt distant from them. Sometimes I felt the conversations were too polite and superficial. Other foreign faculties who taught at my university longer expressed similar feelings when I asked them. My Korean colleagues encouraged me to naturalize. So, since I will live in this country I have decided to naturalize.

Mr. C feels that he made the right decision.

> I perceive that my colleagues accept me more openly, and I myself feel more comfortable in relationships with them. I can relate to them without hesitation and share the same interests.

Mr. C is a good example of a person from a Huaqiao multinational family. Belonging to a multinational family provides the cultural benefit of being able to view the world more in global terms through one's family contacts. He adds,

> I have four younger sisters and also friends living in Taiwan, and I visit Taiwan often. Some of them know that I am naturalized and to those who don't know, I announce that I have become Korean. No one seems too surprised. Rather, the Taiwanese think it is a natural thing to do. They think it is strange that some people try so hard to maintain Taiwanese citizenship rather than being concerned about adapting to the new place we have adopted to live in. It is the same with the [mainland] Chinese. I lived in China for a year and made many friends. The first time I visited China I didn't know much about China but spoke fluent Chinese. I told them that I was a Korean with Chinese ancestry. They were very surprised at my fluency in Chinese, even though I have Chinese ancestors, but not surprised at all about my naturalization. They thought it was natural. Chinese are accustomed to Overseas -Chinese who don't speak Chinese well enough. They [the Chinese] are very accepting of all of them. Whether the Overseas-Chinese seek China or not is up to the individual, but I think the Chinese are very accepting and understanding of those who wish to assimilate into a host society. Most of the Chinese I met were like that, maybe because they have many contacts with Overseas-Chinese.

The opportunity to work after high school graduation also influenced Korean-Huaqiaos to select Korean universities. Further, a higher degree of contact with Korean society, such as attending Korean universities, has resulted in a higher degree of ethnic integration. Ms. K is a second-generation Huaqiao. Upon high school graduation, she worked at a company which does translating, and she felt she needed a college education if she was going to make any advancement in her career. She was easily accepted at a Korean university as an extra-quorum student. She attended the evening division and continued her work during the day. She met her husband at college.

> When we [my husband and I] announced our intentions to marry, both families were opposed. The only reason was because we were of different nationalities.

She said her mother, who is Korean, was opposed to the idea the most.

> My mother didn't want me to follow in her footsteps of adjusting to
> a different culture.

Ms. K said she felt uneasy before getting married, because she felt responsible for representing the Chinese people rather than the Koreans. Contrary to the rumors she had heard about Korean men, her husband is very family-oriented and helps her with household chores. Also, her in-laws are very helpful. She is very happy about her choice to marry a Korean, but she met some other domineering Korean men, and can understand why Chinese parents want their daughters to go to Taiwan to marry Taiwanese men. She mentioned that Huaqiaos believe that life is easy for women in Taiwan, and that Taiwanese men are more gentle than Korean men. The issue about marriage, especially for female students, is also a consideration in college choices. To avoid inter-ethnic marriage, many Huaqiao parents send their daughters to Taiwanese universities. This point will be discussed later.

Ms. K is a naturalized Korean. Her husband is a chief executive in a Korean company, and his work often requires him to travel abroad, so she often accompanies him. She explained that for Taiwanese nationals it is very difficult to get visas from other countries due to the Taiwanese government's limited diplomatic relationships. She travels now because it is much easier to get a visa since she became naturalized. In addition, she did not want her children to be discriminated against or teased because of their mother's Taiwanese nationality. She does not feel any discrimination in everyday life or in legal matters because her husband and in-laws take care of all these things. Her children are studying at a Korean school. She feels that it is important for them [her children] to know about Korea more than China because Korea is their motherland and most likely they will live in Korea.

Among members of the younger generation, a growing number of Huaqiaos have become naturalized Koreans, both through marriage and also independently. An interview with a councelor at the People's Republic of China embassy indicated that China encourages its Huaqiaos to naturalize and adapt to the host society. China will help its expatriates within the scope of its own interests and it does not want diplomatic friction with any country about issues concerning the Huaqiaos.

However, there were and are certain benefits to being a foreigner. For instance, even through Korea's developing economy during the1970s and 1980s restricted travel abroad in order to save precious foreign currencies, the Huaqiaos, as foreign nationals, were not bound by such restrictions and could enjoy overseas travel, which made them the envy of the majority of Koreans. Some even managed small scale international peddling and did well. Education is another arena in which the Huaqiaos benefit from being foreign nationals, as they have more choices in the types of education they can receive in Korea. The Huaqiaos are permitted to organize and operate ethnic schools in Korea, and they can also be educated in Korean schools if they choose. Some well-to-do families send their children to American schools to be educated in English. In contrast to the options the Huaqiaos have, it is compulsory for Korean students to attend Korean schools. The admission of the Huaqiaos to Korean universities without having to take the competitive exam — in a country of "examination hell" — makes the Huaqiaos the envy of every Korean. Reflecting upon this, a few of my interviewees indicated that they have considered naturalization for economic benefits but have decided to wait until their children finish college.

Demographic Background

Korean-Huaqiaos are as homogeneous as the Korean population which they have adopted. A survey completed in October of 1997 by the Overseas Chinese Middle and High Schools indicated that 93.4 percent of the students' places of origin are from Shantung and three percent from Hebei province in China. Only 0.4 percent were reported to originate from the Northeastern provinces. Korean-Huaqiaos largely came from two villages in Shantung, which is across from Inchon, the port of arrival for the majority of the immigrants. These statistics indicate that the major source of migration was through kinship and hometown networks, as is also the case of Huaqiaos with the Southeast Asian countries. The geographical proximity of these villages to Inchon is exaggerated in a quip that states, "from Inchon one could hear a rooster crowing" in those villages of their hometown. Naturally, this geographical proximity enabled many Huaqiaos to move easily to Korea. Since Shantung is located near Beijing, the Huaqiao population in Korea speaks the Shantung dialect, which is very close to standard Chinese.

Korean-Huaqiaos are a largely urban population. The survey at the Seoul Overseas Chinese High School indicated that sixty percent of the students were from Seoul. Of the remaining students, nine percent were from Kyungki province, fifteen percent from Kangwon province, seventeen percent from Chungbuk province, twenty-seven percent from Chungnam, and fifteen percent from Jeonbuk province (all provinces near Seoul). Jeonnam, Kyungnam, Kyungbuk, and Cheju provinces showed insignificant numbers, perhaps due to the existence of Deagu and Pusan Huaqiao High Schools, which are closer to these provinces. Also, many of the students from the Inchon area attend Inchon Huaqiao High School. Inchon is a port city about one hour from Seoul. With Seoul ever expanding, Inchon has become its satellite city. In 1998, there were 170 Huaqiao senior school students in Seoul, forty-eight in Inchon, forty-eight in Pusan, and twenty-three in Daegu Huaqiao senior high schools (Korea Huaqiao School Teachers' Association, 1998).

Chinese restaurants are the occupation most heavily represented by the ethnic Chinese in Korea. Forty-six percent of the students' parents work in restaurants, usually as owners but also as cooks, and 9.5 percent are hired as cooks. Therefore, more than half of the Huaqiao population in Korea is engaged in the Chinese restaurant business. The concentration of workers in the Chinese restaurant business and retail business is more intense when considering the country as a whole. According to a Huaqiao source, approximately eighty percent of Huaqiao households are engaged in the restaurant business in some way. I will discuss the impact of this concentration later.

The next most popular occupation, eleven percent, is in trade. Four percent are reportedly engaged in traditionally popular Chinese medicine, and four percent in tourism and hospitality. The remainder of the population is engaged in various sales and service industries, while one percent is in agriculture. This low percentage of agricultural workers is due to the Korean government's restriction on ownership of land by foreign nationals. Other modern professions in which the ethnic Chinese participate are two percent each in teaching and government employment [Taiwan], one percent in pharmacy, and 0.5 percent in Western medicine (Seoul Overseas Middle and High School, 1997). Most of the employment opportunities are limited to ethnic community.

Korean-Huaqiaos are multinational families. The survey indicated that forty-three percent of SOCHS graduating seniors of 1998 had family members in one foreign country, thirty-nine percent in two countries, and thirteen percent in three or more countries. Only five percent indicated that they had no family members or relations abroad. Sixty-nine percent of the respondents reported having families and close relatives in Taiwan, followed by forty-four percent in the United States, fifteen percent in China, and thirteen percent in Japan. Various Southeast Asian countries and Australia were mentioned also. At the same time, many of the Huaqiaos reestablished their contacts with relatives in China as soon as diplomatic relations between China and Korea were normalized, and they frequently visit China and do business there. Contact had not been possible since the Korean War due to political enmity between the two countries.

The generation gap is apparent among the Huaqiaos. The interview results suggest that the older generation, especially first-generation immigrants, display strong nostalgia for and attachment to China. Some of the older Huaqiaos revealed their plan to go back to that country. Such an example is Mr. G, who came to Korea in his teens. Now a retired chef, he was as a young man apprenticed to the master chef of "Asawon," probably the most famous Chinese restaurant in Korea during the Japanese colonial period and up until the mid 1970s when it closed. In his prime Mr. G served as on-call cook for former president Park Chung-Hee. Today he can live comfortably on his savings. Younger generation family members are too busy to see him, and other than on occasions when he to meets with his hometown friends in Korea, he spends his retired days alone, which makes him more homesick for China. He has visited China twice and met his old family members and childhood friends. He said he feels right at home and now plans to return there. He realizes that he needs to make a great deal of readjustment as he is used to the Korean standard of living, an area in which China lags behind at the moment. Also, as an Overseas-Chinese he must pay as foreigners do in China, which will make his cost of living very expensive. Still, he is determined to go back home and be buried with his ancestors when he dies. He has a Taiwanese passport now and will change to a Chinese one if necessary. He contends that it was not his political inclination to acquire a Taiwanese passport but rather the political circumstances of the time. He maintains that he simply wants to go home, and there is no political connotation to his wishes.

On the other hand, members of the younger generations are more ambivalent toward China. While the young Huaqiaos recognize some connection to China, they express difficulties in relating to that country. Ms. H states:

> For some 40 years we [the Chinese in Korea and the Chinese in China] lived in a different world. I have my sisters living in Taiwan and some closer members of my husband's family are living there too. But in China, yes, we have relations but haven't seen them for forty some years, so it is not like seeing them often and building a human relationship. . . . I have a half brother, an aunt and some other relations there but I didn't see them while I was growing up and it is difficult to relate to them now. . . . All of a sudden. . . . We don't seem to have any common culture.

On the other hand, through their education young Huaqiaos are more firmly linked to Taiwan. The majority of students consider Taiwan as their motherland, and they attribute their emotional ties to the country to the influence of the Taiwanese-style education they received throughout elementary and secondary school in Korea. The Taiwanese system of education, the Huaqiaos conceded, familiarizes them with the Taiwanese way of life, while China is the distant home of their parents. Another interviewee adds:

> It has much to do with the education we have received so far. . . . I think for most of us China is our ancestral land but Taiwan is our motherland. It is because we are nourished by their education.

The situation with adults is a bit more complex. A statement made by a diplomat at the Taipei Mission illustrates the situation very well.

> The Chinese are very practical people. They are not concerned with politics or ideology. They are only interested in profit. Right now it is in their interest to wait and see the developments. When the decision must be made, it will be made according to their interests. They are not too emotional about the issues of China and Taiwan. They are happy now because they can enjoy both Taiwanese financial support and China's international prestige.

Due to Taiwanese-influenced education and their cultural contacts during the past forty years, most of the younger generation Huaqiaos in Korea are much more familiar with and prefer the Taiwanese way of life, as reflected in the students' responses in the survey, which asked their opinion about the national characteristics of China, Korea, and Taiwan. Students absolutely agreed on China's superiority in historical and cultural heritage, the natural environment and resources, culture and art, and potential future development. On the other hand, Taiwan was viewed as having strength in science and technology, higher standard in education, social welfare, social stability, and democracy. The students in general thought that their life would be improved if they lived in Taiwan, while China was described as the place they least desired to live. They explained the seeming inconsistency between pride in China's cultural and historical heritage and the fact that it was the least desired place to live as due to the economic backwardness and the low standard of living at this time. Everyone seemed confident that China would catch up with Korea very soon. Also, they indicated Taiwan was the country for which they have patriotic feelings and which they are willing to serve. Korea was ranked as average in the areas of science and technology, social welfare, and democracy.

Still, some older generation Huaqiaos showed enthusiasm toward China, claiming that the Huaqiaos' legal position in Korea, such as reentry visa and permission of residency, had improved since Korea's diplomatic opening with China in 1992. Some Huaqiaos believe that this is because of China's international strength, which Taiwan lacks. According to an interviewee:

> Taiwan was afraid to speak to the Korean government on our behalf. As a result, we [Huaqiaos] suffered. Nothing has ever been done. Huaqiaos have been living in Korea for generations, and we must renew our residency permit every three years, and when traveling abroad we only get a one-year, single entry visa. China is a big country. There has been improvement already. Now, a residency permit is five years and a travel visa is for three years, multiple entry. If the Chinese ambassador requests a meeting with the Minister of Foreign Affairs of Korea, most likely he will make time. I doubt he [the Korean Foreign Minster] would have given the same consideration to the Taiwanese ambassador. . . .There is no opportunity in Korea for the educated Huaqiao youth. I tell everyone that they must go abroad if they wish to become successful.

Yet others maintain that the friendly relationship between the Korean and Taiwanese governments enabled Korean-Huaqiaos to live relatively free in Korea. An official from Taipei Mission informed me that there is only one person who changed his nationality from Taiwan to China since 1992, when the choice was given to Korean-Huaqiaos to either maintain their Taiwanese nationality or to change it to China. The majority of Huaqiaos in Korea choose to remain Taiwanese while reopening their contacts with China. Yet, Taiwan fever seems to be cooling down among Korean-Huaqiaos, and there are hints of conflict within the Huaqiao community. Shim observed in his report in the *Far Eastern Economic Review* (1992) that the solidarity of the Chinese community in Korea deteriorated as the two camps, pro-Taiwan and pro-China, developed at the time of the diplomatic switch-over. His observation is validated by my fieldwork. I often heard Huaqiaos referring to someone as either "pro-Taiwan" or "pro-China," a manner in which people also aligned themselves.

Chapter Five

Chinese Immigration to Korea and the Social and Economic History of the Korean-Huaqiaos

Noting that "history is self-exploration" Ken Burns observed that

> The question that we ask of the past, which is called history, are questions we ask in the present, so that history has the possibility of becoming a kind of medicine that can teach us about ourselves as well as teach us about distant times. The questions we ask of those distant times are questions that we today need to have answered. And that's an important thing to remember: that history is not propaganda, history is not a weapon, history is not the truth. But history is a way of self, and I mean that at both the largest societal level and at the deeply, intensely personal, psychological level.

Wang (1981) construes history as

> There are two different ways the word 'history' may be used. Both refer to the past, but one describes our knowledge or perception of the past and the other the actions and developments which have already taken place in the past (p. 1)

The presence of ethnic Chinese in Korea and their relationship to Korean society requires a historical focus as "historical analysis sheds much light on contemporary patterns and trends" (Bray and Lee 1997, p. 5). The history of Chinese immigration to Korea is closely related to modern Korean history. All the events of Korea's recent past, such as the Sino-Japanese War, which took place on the Korean peninsula, the Japanese colonial period, Korean Independence, the subsequent division of the country into South Korea (Republic of Korea) and North

Korea (People's Republic of Korea), and the Korean War, shaped the characteristics of Korean-Huaqiaos. The different political and economic situations of Korea, China, and Taiwan influenced the status of the ethnic Chinese and their relationships with the Korean people. Chinese migration can be found in the political, economic, and historical realities of the countries involved in Korea's affairs at various times, and can be broadly divided into three eras: 1) The end of the Chosun Dynasty (1882-1910); 2) The Japanese Colonial Period (1910-1945); 3) Post-Korean Independence (1945 to present). It appears that a new relationship has been emerging between Korea and the Korean-Huaqiaos since 1992 with the normalization of diplomatic ties between Korea and China.

The End of the Chosun Period (1882-1910)

In the late nineteenth century, China's role in Korea, which was limited to political influence, was rapidly waning, while the newly industrialized Japan's colonial ambition in Korea was steadily increasing. It was at that point in time when the Chinese people's immigration to Korea began. The Immo military mutiny (1882), a military revolt against Japanese encroachment in Korea, brought 4,000 Chinese soldiers and 40 Chinese merchants to the country at the request of the Korean King, Kojong, who sought the presence of the Chinese military to counterbalance the rising Japanese influence. Chinese soldiers soon withdrew, but some of the merchants returned and began to conduct trade. Due to Korea's earlier political subordination to China, these merchants had an unfair economic advantage over Korean merchants. At the urging of the Chinese government, successive trade treaties were concluded between the two countries. These agreements were advantageous to Chinese merchants and facilitated the continuous migration of the Chinese into Korea. The Chinese population in Korea reached 11,818 in 1910, up from 209 in 1883 (see population table).

Although Chinese involvement in Korea did not lead to the formation of a colonial government there, during this period the Chinese behaved like a colonial power toward Korea. The Chinese community was beyond Korean police control, and the Chinese enjoyed superior social status and economic opportunities in Korean society because the Chinese government continued to pressure the weak Korean government for preferential treatment of the Chinese people there (Park 1986). Consequently, ordinary Koreans suffered from the oppressive attitudes of the Chinese on their own soil.

Along with these lopsided power relations came asymmetrical economic relations. The Chinese held a superior position in the area of trade, since most foreign products were entering Korea through China. The Chinese in Korea made maximum use of their ethnic backgrounds, supplying wealthy Koreans with Chinese silk, textiles, and other European goods. Goods imported from and through China increased year after year and were distributed throughout Korea. Economic specialization occurred: the Chinese in commerce and Koreans in agriculture. While Korean society was divided between the scholarly/gentry class and the peasant majority, the Chinese began to form a mercantile class (Park, 1986).

The Japanese Colonial Period (1910-1945)

After Japan's annexation of Korea in 1910, Japanese colonial officials controlled the social, cultural, political, and economic activities of the entire population of that country. Koreans and Chinese alike were under Japanese control. As in the case of other Southeast Asian countries under colonial rule, the ethnic Chinese in Korea did not see the benefit of associating with Koreans, thereby preventing an integration of the minority and majority populations during this time. The two societies remained separate.

As the Japanese attempted to extract maximum profits by exploiting Korea through industry and trade, both the Koreans and the Chinese were placed at a disadvantage. Japan brought its own capital into Korea, combining it with Korean natural resources, electricity, and cheap labor. At the same time, the Japanese colonial authorities attempted to gain the upper hand economically by restricting the superior trading role of the Chinese in Korea. Japan instituted a new economic policy that included added tariffs imposed on the goods imported from China. Yet, the Chinese trade network continued to control the Korean market through distribution of goods. The nationwide trade network dominated by the Chinese, including retailers and peddlers of imported textiles and other products, not only survived but thrived, and the Japanese were not able to compete commercially with the Chinese (Park, 1986).

Korea as a colonized country could not look out for its own best interests. So the Japanese managed Chinese immigration policies in Korea to maximize their own colonial aims. Sometimes, Japan permitted Chinese immigration into Korea in order to solicit cheap labor and buy off Korean land from displaced peasants, while at other times they restricted immigration to contain economic chaos.

Whereas earlier the Chinese in Korea instituted the mercantile class, during the Japanese colonial period, three notable historical forces started to draw other Chinese populations to the country. At the end of the Qing dynasty (1644-1911/2), much social and political unrest occurred in China. For example, the Chinese people's resentment of foreign infringement into their country led to the Boxer Rebellion (1900). But the revolt failed, causing disillusionment and, furthermore, making the population the subject of retaliation by the foreign powers in control of China. As a result, masses of peasants, fearing for their lives, immigrated to Korea. Simultaneously, the political instability of the weakened Qing government made leaders unable to control bandits, mobs, and other undesirable elements, and the social unrest became a threat to daily living. For the Chinese populace, afraid to live in this state of anarchy without protection, Korea was the nearest place for them and a natural destination. A third factor that prompted people to emmigrate from China was the country's high population density and the added burden of continuous natural disasters such as floods and famines, which caused two to three million deaths by starvation. Thus, there were two distinct characteristics of early Huaqiaos in Korea: first, the population was heavily concentrated in urban areas, and, second, there was a high male to female ratio, the social impact of which I will discuss later.

The three most general routes by which the Chinese came to Korea were 1) a direct move from Shantung to Inchon by sea and then a dispersal to other areas; 2) a move to Korea from or through Manchuria by land; and 3) through Japan. The first route was the most popular. The remarks of interviewees highlight the routes along which the Chinese chose to emmigrate as well as their motives for leaving China. A second-generation interviewee, who is, the editor of an ethnic daily newspaper, relates,

> My father came around 1930 because people were starving to death in China. He came through Inchon and worked as a laborer. That was the case for most Huaqiaos coming to Korea then. My father said he saw rice for the first time in his life in Korea. The situation in China was so poor that many people dried cooked rice [Koreans call it *nurunggi*] and in this way the weight becomes lighter to carry, and sent it to China with someone when they were visiting at home. Many families were nourished throughout the year with the dried cooked rice that had been sent from Korea.

Another interviewee commented,

> I am a second-generation Huaqiao and my teenage children are third generation. My father came to avoid the draft by the Red Army. My grandmother urged him to leave [China]. First, he went to Manchuria and then proceeded to Korea. He was married in

China, but he came alone and married my mother after the Korean War [when he could not return to China].

Mr. Z's father is one of the most recent immigrants to Korea.

My father deserted the People's Liberation Army during the Korean War. He said he simply walked out. He said he felt he had no choice between either getting shot trying to escape or dying of starvation in the People's Army. They were sent to the front without being given a gun or any kind of ammunition . . . There are several of them [Huaqiaos] like my father [in Korea].

During this time, Korean-Huaqiaos preferred to remit their savings to China or to invest and thereby accumulate their money in business enterprises, which kept their capital relatively liquid and left it available to be turned over quickly. With family members still in China, many Chinese had emigrated temporarily, so they saved money with the idea of returning home when the situation there had improved. Since movement between Korea and China was relatively free, many Chinese did business in Korea, occasionally returning home to China to visit relatives during holidays (Park, 1986). The Chinese in Korea were, therefore, sojourners with no intention of relocating to Korea permanently. Their interests were purely economic. Many similar characteristics have been detected between the Chinese in Korea and the Chinese in Southeast Asian countries. According to Ooda, in 1922, fifty-two percent of the Chinese in Korea engaged in trade, seventeen percent in farming, and thirty percent in labor (cited in Park, 1986). These statistics reflect that as newly arrived migrants the Huaqiaos in Korea were urban dwellers. Korean-Huaqiaos are still today largely engaged in small entrepreneurships, as is the case with many Huaqiaos in Southeast Asian countries.

The urban base of the immigrant Chinese community dominated nearly all large city centers in Korea, and also gave the ethnic population an advantage over the rural-based Korean population as far as access to markets, marketing information, and trading contacts. Park (1986) attributes the commercial success of Korean-Huaqiaos during this time to mobilization of resources through a credit and apprentice system. At the same time, she concedes that personal attributes such as frugality, diligence, and endurance were also important in the Huaqiaos' commercial success. Through kinship hometown connections and a rotating credit system, the Chinese mobilized credit which was not available to Koreans. It should be noted that Huaqiaos in Korea had fewer opportunities than their Southeast Asian Chinese counterparts to act as agents for larger colonial commercial enterprises. Yet, middleman activities in rural areas often developed as a vertical extension of larger scale Chinese businesses in the towns. Park (1986) credits the commercial success of the ethnic Chinese to their efficiency and reliability. The Chinese often offered more favorable terms of credit than Koreans did, and the Chinese merchants were more concerned with establishing long-term commitments with their clients rather than maximizing short-term gains. Park further notes that this type of business practice was possible through an ethnic credit system. Interviews revealed that apprentices were brought to Korea through kinship or hometown connections when they were young, and that they were trained thoroughly by the employer, who acted as a guardian, saved the apprentice's wages, and set up a shop for the young person after he completed his apprenticeship. The fact that those who paid the highest taxes during the Japanese colonial period were the Chinese demonstrates their outstanding success (Park, 1986).

Lim (1986) contends that trade was an obvious occupation for investment by these ethnic minorities, who were barred from other traditional occupations by the host population. Commercial production and market exchange in particular were just developing on a wide scale when the Chinese came to Korea and offered many opportunities for middleman activities that often required relatively little capital. Koreans, "having access to land but little access either to capital or to growing urban and international markets, remained in agricultural production, leaving the urban-based Chinese immigrants to fill the vacuum in trade, marketing, commerce, and service occupations" (Hafner, 1986; Gosling, 1986).

China was experiencing long term political turmoil, which produced a new government in 1911, and this historical development caused the further migration of Chinese into Korea. This new regime was not strong enough, however, to control the whole of China nor to eradicate the infamous local bandits of the Shantung area. A related political problem was the Japanese invasion and the conflict between the communists and KMT both of which frequently raided villages. To make matters worse, natural disasters such as floods and famines occurred during the 1920s. Subsequently, the next surge of ethnic Chinese, mostly of peasant origin, arrived in the Korean peninsula in the 1930s. These Chinese laborers were often used as strike breakers. This influx of workers contributed to the rise of economic refugees in Korea, as the Chinese competed for cheaper labor (Park, 1986).

The Republic of China was founded in 1912 with the collapse of the Qing dynasty. In 1921, the Chinese Communist Party was established and afterward the country was generally divided into two rivaling factions: the Nationalist Party (KMT) and the Communist Party (CCP). The Japanese invasion of China forged a temporary alliance between the KMT and CCP. This alliance soon collapsed and the country was in chaos. In 1949, after its defeat in the Sino-Japanese War and its overthrow by the Communist Party, the KMT government retreated to Taiwan. Thus, the Huaqiaos who migrated to Korea while the Republic of China was in power were recognized as ROC nationals.

Taiwan attempted to solicit the patriotism of Overseas-Chinese through education. During the booming economy and when the KMT was in power financial and educational incentives were available. However, the stabile economy made it hard to create new jobs and Taiwan had to cater to its own people first. The growing power of separatists reflected the Taiwanese sentiment of "Taiwanese first." All these developments meant less opportunity for the Huaqiaos in Taiwan

Chin notes that these laborers worked under headmen. Mostly single males, these headmen had advantages over Korean laborers in wage competition. Chin (1979) recounted that these laborers were only sustained by a couple of dumplings a day, had only two pairs of clothing, and mostly shared one room with many people. A headman often had ten to thirty laborers under him, and he negotiated their wages and working conditions and often saved the laborers' wages for them until their contract was up. Although there were certain cases in which some of these headmen exploited and abused the laborers, most of these arrangements worked out well. With their savings the laborers were able to engage in entrepreneurship. Park (1986) observes that these types of arrangements were advantageous and worked as collective bargaining. The immigrants' urban base and social networks, established for mutual support in strange lands, provided access to market information, cheap capital, and labor.

In areas where the Chinese engaged in agricultural production, they again filled a vacuum not occupied by Koreans. Chin (1979) describes how some Chinese peasants participated in market agriculture and supplied produced goods to an increasingly urbanized city population. Hefner (1986) points out that the Chinese market gardeners in Thailand occupied saline tidal tracts and gulf margins not suitable for Thai rice growing, which expanded inland along alluvial plains. Hefner explains that for Teochiu and Hainanese farmers, however, these ecological conditions were similar to those they faced in South China. In Korea also, the urban focus of early Chinese residence and employment enabled these farmers to establish the required market ties to the growing urban market of Seoul. Urban merchants, traders, and even secret societies helped finance the production and marketing of vegetables and fruit by Chinese farmers (Chin, 1979). This practice is in stark contrast to subsistence farming by Koreans.

Post-Korean Independence (1945-Present)

Korean independence brought drastic changes in the relationship between the Koreans and the Chinese: Koreans became nationals of a sovereign state and the Chinese were regarded as residing foreigners. Naturally, their legal status as foreigners in a newly independent country placed the Huaqiaos in Korea at a disadvantage, for Korean laws focused on the interests of Koreans. The Huaqiaos' subordinate position was reflected in their lack of access to land for farming and their restriction from certain occupations, which made self-employment in petty trade virtually the only means for upward mobility from low-wage employment.

By the time the Korean War broke out in 1950, there were some 40,000 ethnic Chinese in Korea, who had already established thriving businesses. The war and the subsequent division of Korea decreased the Korean-Chinese population again. Historically, the two regions of Korea have been interdependent — the north had a more commercial and industrial base, while the south provided agricultural products; therefore, greater numbers of Chinese resided in the north. With the division of Korea, neither the Chinese nor the Korean population could travel back and forth any longer between the two regions. After the Korean Armistice, the South Korean government, burdened with its own population explosion, restricted immigration. Also, as a result of China's active support of North Korea in the Korean War, political hostility arose between China and South Korea, which prohibited further movement and/or contacts between the Huaqiaos and China. Thus, from this time on, the Huaqiao population in Korea increased through births, with many Huaqiaos having a Korean mother and a Chinese father. By the 1960s, the number of ethnic Chinese in South Korea soared to 50,000, but in the 1970s the Huaqiao population there began to decrease again. The first decrease occurred during the 1930s, after the Manbosan Mt. Incident (an ethnic clash between Koreans and Chinese), which occurred in Manchuria. However, this tension soon settled as Koreans and Chinese began to realize that the Japanese had instigated the incident. Many Huaqiaos during 1970s and 1980s moved to Taiwan, the United States, and other countries.

Huaqiaos claim that these emigrations of their people to other countries were due to inhospitable Korean policies, such as the Korean government's immediate concern about the country's economic development. New Korean policies often neglected the Huaqiaos' welfare, and both indirect and direct discrimination adversely affected the Chinese community. In addition, Korea, emerging from a colonial past, felt uneasy about an ethnic minority having economic and political power which might undermine the nation's interests. Economically, the government's restrictions on foreign exchange hit the Chinese trade business in a critical way. As foreign nationals Huaqiaos were prohibited from owning land. Another way in which the Chinese were affected was that they could not have the benefit of receiving a favorable exchange rate in foreign trade. Huaqiao traders, therefore, had to use the black market exchange rate, which was about two or three times higher than the official rate. Along with the loss of trading sources in China, the handicap of foreign exchange undermined the Huaqiaos' trade business in Korea. In addition to the unfavorable foreign exchange rate, the Huaqiaos also had to suffer the burden of the new law prohibiting foreigners from forming a new company. Further, commercial bank loans were not easily available to them. To overcome this discrimination and unfavorable business climate, some wealthy Huaqiaos went into partnership with Koreans, but most of these alliances turned out to be disastrous and many disputes developed. Hence, during the 1950s, many Huaqiaos changed their occupations from commerce to small-scale entrepreneurships focusing mainly on the restaurant business. According to traditional Korean values, commerce is not respected because it was seen as parasitical and non-productive. The restaurant business was viewed in an even more negative light by Korean society. However, as immigrants who had no social position, the ethnic Chinese were less constrained by such social restraints. For them, making money was the only route to success. Easily acquired cooking skills, small amounts of capital, and the negative attitude of Koreans toward the restaurant business led to the Korean-Huaqiaos almost monopolizing the restaurant business, which flourished, and to Huaqiaos being identified with the food industry. In 1948, there were only 332 Chinese restaurants, but the number reached 1,636 in 1962, and 2,464 in 1972, the year in which year seventy-seven percent of the total Huaqiao households in Korea were operating restaurants (Park, 1986).

As Korean society rapidly industrialized during the 1970s, the values and lifestyle of Koreans changed so that commerce and merchants were no longer seen as an inferior. As a result, the society's perceptions of the restaurant business or commercial activity became more positive. Economic affluence also altered people's attitude toward dining. As people began dining out more frequently, they began to seek variety in cuisine, with the result that now the Chinese restaurants were receiving more competition from the Koreans. A shortage of Huaqiao labor, caused by the lack of a new flow of Chinese immigration, dictated the hiring of Koreans for kitchen help and delivery, which was not a traditional Chinese practice. These Koreans soon became competitors, as they began their own restaurants with the skills they had acquired during their employment, and developed cooking techniques better suited to Koreans' tastes. These Korean restauranteurs also invested lavishly in the interior of their enterprises to attract Korean customers, and began to compete with traditionally managed and humbly decorated Huaqiao restaurants. Further, some of the Huaqiaos lost their downtown business locations to massive urban planning throughout Korea in the 1970s. Having given up their businesses, many Huaqiaos migrated to the United States, Taiwan, and other countries during this period. The United States Immigration Act of 1965, which abolished the quota system, coincided with this outflow. By 1981, the Chinese population in Korea decreased to 28,717, a thirteen percent decrease from 1972. The Chinese social and economic network weakened as relatives and friends moved out of Korea, which in turn forced even more people to leave the country.

As such, the Korean government's urban planning policies from the 1970s through the 1980s resulted in the residential disintegration of the Chinese communities and caused the disappearance of Chinatowns (*Chosen Daily*, July 27, August 7, 1991; *Sekye Daily*, April 26, 27, 1991; *Korea Daily*, March 27, 1991). Various newspapers claimed that the government's urban planning and its economic favoritism of Korean businesses forced many ethnic Chinese to leave Korea, thus decreasing the Huaqiao population. While there was now more integration between Koreans and the ethnic Chinese in Korean society, community support within the minority group was lessened as a result, which undermined the preservation of the Chinese language and cultural heritage, and, in turn, weakened ethnic identity.

Huaqiaos all agree that 1992 represents a turning point for them in Korea, and that important changes were brought about by the Korean government's shift to a diplomatic relationship with China, away from Taiwan. Encouraged by its economic success, Korea launched the Northern Politic, which opened up diplomatic relations with former communist countries, most notably China and Russia. This was a drastic change from the Korean government's prior staunch anti-communism policies. The normalization of diplomatic relations between South Korea (ROK) and China (PRC) took place in 1992. Korea's diplomatic shift away from Taiwan, was significant to the Huaqiaos in Korea, who had their ancestral homeland and relatives in China but who had adopted Taiwan as their motherland over the previous forty years. With this opening of diplomatic relations, the Huaqiaos in Korea were now able to visit China without fear of discovery by Korean (and perhaps Taiwanese) Intelligence, while at the same time maintaining their relationship with Taiwan. The ethnic Chinese thus had greater options and opportunities. Some suggest that this important change brought the deterioration of solidarity within the Chinese community in Korea, leading to the formation of a pro-Taiwan and a pro-China camp (*Far

Eastern Economic Review, 1992). Although there is some truth in this suggestion, most Huaqiaos appear to be apolitical and to enjoy the broadened opportunities. While acknowledging the importance of these expanded horizons, many Huaqiaos began to consider remaining in Korea as more attractive because they were able to freely visit their relations and to conduct business in China, enjoying their strong ethnic connection, language, and culture while maintaining their familiar lifestyle in their host country.

The growing power of the Korean-Huaqiaos can be seen in the reemergence of Chinatowns in Korea. Recently, there have been signs of an upsurge in Chinatowns in the Sedaemoon area of Yun-nam dong and Hongchon dong, near the Seoul Overseas Chinese High School. The revitalized Chinatowns differ from those of the past. In contrast to the formally ghetto-like, commercially oriented locations, the new areas contain residential dwellings and business offices (*Jungang Daily*, December 7, 1996; *Chosen Daily*, January 28, October 16, 17, 1996), perhaps in a way reflecting recent trends among the Huaqiao population. There are a growing number of younger-generation Huaqiaos in white collar professions, and even those who own restaurants or small shops prefer to commute to work from their homes. This presented a change in attitude from that of previous generations whose work place and residence were often the same, a practice that was economical but less suited to family life. In Inchon, the city government is supporting the restoration of historical Chinatown (*Chosen Daily*, Regional Edition, November 15, 1995; *Chosen Daily*, January 28, 1996). These revivals of Chinatowns seem to reflect positive changes for the ethnic Chinese population in Korea, where political maturity and economic progress seem to have created room for ethnic coexistence.

These positive signs of growth are reflected in the college preference of the Huaqiao youth. In the past, Taiwanese universities were popular, but now the majority of students are entering Korean universities. According to a Huaqiao community leader,

> Since 1992, the Chinese community has been experiencing a setback due to not being able to adjust to changes. We are in a transitional period, but the Chinese community is not coming up with any solution to meet this change. There is no centripetal point in the Huaqiao community in Korea. In the past, the Taiwanese government supported us in every aspect, including educational matters. Since 1992, we are experiencing a change in attitude and policy on the part of the Taiwan government. Regardless of our ideology, China is our home, not our own but that of our parents; we

speak the same language and have relatives there. Of course, we are and want to be on friendly terms with China. Realizing this, Taiwan understands our situation. One outcome [since 1992], I think, is the change in the entrance into Korean universities [by Korean-Huaqiao youth], and we encourage them that way. In the past, fewer than one-third went to Korean universities, while more than two-thirds went to Taiwanese universities. Now it is changing, and most of the students are entering Korean universities.

The details of college choices will be discussed later.

Economic Arena

Lim (1986) attributes Chinese dominance in particular kinds of economic activity, especially in trade and commerce in Southeast Asia, to a variety of historical, structural, social, and cultural factors. She notes that as landless, foreign wage laborers employed in mines, plantations, and towns, Chinese immigrants generally did not have access to the traditional occupations of indigenous populations, mainly farming rice for subsistence, and later, for commercial production. Due to the exclusion of the Chinese from owning land for farming or other productive activities, as happened from time to time in various countries, the Huaqiaos became urban dwellers where the information flow is swift. Lim's insightful observations about the Southeast Asian Huaqiaos are also useful in investigating the Korean-Chinese. As in the case of the Southeast Asian countries, the Korean-Huaqiaos are largely small entrepreneurs and, as a result, mostly urban-based. An explanation can be found in their legal status as "alien," which handicapped the economic activities of Huaqiaos in Korea as elsewhere. The new laws and policies placed Koreans at an advantage when competing with non-nationals. Huaqiaos, therefore, were often either overlooked or indirectly or directly discriminated against in their economic pursuits.

As stated earlier, there was an exodus of Huaqiao students to Taiwan from Korea from the 1960s through the early 1980s. According to the interviewees, who unanimously agreed, the economic policies of the Korean government in the past were the single most important explanation for the Korean-Huaqiao students' decision to leave Korea. I continually heard the following comments when interviewing them about economic issues:

> There are too many restrictions for the Korean-Huaqiaos. We can't get jobs because we are not Koreans, and even when we get jobs, we are not promoted; certain occupations such as law and trade we

cannot engage in, we pay higher taxes, even ownership of property
is limited . . .

Therefore, Korean-Huaqiaos feel that "Korean prosperity does not include us" and that "Korea is a good place to live if you are a Korean."

Naturally, Taiwan became more attractive as it offered minimal taxes for small businesses and reduced tuition for Huaqiao students in postsecondary education. Korean-Huaqiaos used admission to Taiwanese universities as a means to emigrate to Taiwan. Examining the Korean government's economic policies will aid in the understanding of this issue.

Huaqiaos blame the oppression they experienced on the Korean government's antagonistic policies toward the ethnic Chinese that began in 1958, and that systematically put the interests of Koreans before those of foreign nationals. Both President Syngman Rhee (1948-1960) and Park Chung-Hee (1961-1979) launched currency reforms, some of which were announced suddenly and left people who failed to convert their cash in time, with worthless notes. The time-honored Chinese tradition of stashing cash away was profoundly affected by these reforms, which contributed to the economic decline of the Korean-Huaqiaos. Moreover, the Korean tax system at that time worked against this minority. The government even regulated the prices Chinese restaurants could charge. In 1961, the Korean government introduced a law that required foreigners who owned land to seek approval from the Minister of Interior within a year. Many Korean-Huaqiaos failed to get approval and were forced to sell, and Huaqiao farmers had to change their occupations, as they were no longer allowed to own land. Most of the farmers who were displaced from their land due to the prohibition became small entrepreneurs, mostly entering into the restaurant business or running small retail shops. These changes brought further urbanization of the Huaqiaos. The prohibition against land-owning by foreign nationals was abolished in 1993; however, other restrictions on foreigners owning land still remained until 1998. In 1998, Korea was also affected by the Asian financial crisis, and the country was placed under the guidance of the International Monetary Fund (IMF). Many of the restrictions were abrogated at that time in order to attract foreign investment. This study is limited to the time prior to the 1998 financial crisis.

The closing of warehouses and the restrictions on foreign exchange in the spring of 1950 caused additional financial damage to the Huaqiaos. The Korean government's rationale for these policies was to eradicate the illegal import of foreign goods. Huaqiao sources claim that these policies were intended to restrict their people's foreign trade activities by allowing trading companies that were owned by Korean nationals a favorable exchange allocation, while Huaqiaos had to resort to the black market, which was two to three times higher than the official rate. Some Huaqiaos went into joint ventures with Koreans to avoid these legal restrictions — Koreans as the legal owners, and Huaqiaos as the providers of capital and the managers of the business — similar to that of "Alibaba cooperation" (Malaysian legal ownership with Chinese capital and management in business) in Indonesia or Malaysia. For a foreigner to acquire a business permit, first, one had to obtain a permission from the Minister of Industry and Energy, and then from the Minister of Commerce and Trade, while Korean nationals simply had to register. These ventures often failed because of legal disputes, and thus the Huaqiaos' foreign trade decreased. This practice of registering the firms in the name of Korean nationals was used in other enterprises such as factories and newspapers, because it had the double advantage of easy registration and lower tax burdens.

The Huaqiaos' economic situation worsened when Park Chung-Hee came to power. The Huaqiaos believe that currency reform in 1961 was aimed at them in order to dismantle their economic power. The prohibition of ownership of real estate by foreign nationals followed. With the promulgation of this law, many Huaqiaos were in danger of losing their homes. Some avoided the catastrophe by placing the title of their homes in the names of Korean friends. This law was amended in 1968 to allow foreign individuals of more than five years residence with a visa (F-2 visa) to acquire 200 pyung (one pyung is equivalent to 3.24 square meters) of land for residence, fifty pyung of land for commerce, and 200 pyung of land for a complex building of residence and commerce. But the process was irksome, and it placed an additional burden on foreign nationals who wished to purchase real estate property. In order to acquire land, one had to obtain approval from the mayor or the provincial governor of the land site. This request for permission would be either granted or rejected within sixty days. However, for Koreans it took less than a month to conclude a contract.

This restriction was intended to restrain speculative investment in real estate, which was prevalent throughout the country in the 1970s and 1980s. In response to these ventures, the Korean government applied anti-speculative measures, such as the Residential Land Holding Ceiling System and the Restrictions on the Lotting-out Price of Apartments. The Huaqiaos are bitter about these measures that not only caused them a variety of inconveniences in their lives and business activities but also striped away their economic opportunity. In Korea, where inflation was high, investing in real estate was used as a secure way to accumulate means. One interviewee indignantly said:

> My Korean friends who were from the same socio-economic back-
> ground are now much better off than I am. The difference is that
> they are Koreans and I am Huaqiao. As Koreans they were allowed
> to invest in anything, including a house. That was not allowed to
> me. I am a third-generation Huaqiao, and that makes my children
> fourth generation since we came to Korea. I have lived in Korea all
> my life except for the time when I was in college in Taiwan. I was
> deprived of the basic rights to which all human beings are entitled.
> Now, even with my lifelong work, I cannot afford a house in which
> I can retire.

Another Huaqiao I interviewed sounded very agitated:

> Do tell me! Can you do business in a 162 square meter shop?
> Nowadays, without a parking lot, how can you do business? But the
> concern for a parking lot is a luxury to us. Where would you furnish
> the office and where would you stock the merchandise?

Interviews revealed that some wealthy Huaqiaos became naturalized to
avoid such legal bindings.

Huaqiaos feel that they were also mistreated by the Seoul metropolitan government, which announced redevelopment plans in 1973.
Chinatown, where many of the Huaqiaos' living and working areas
were located, is in the heart of downtown Seoul. In some of the development zones landowners were required to build high-rise buildings.
Many Huaqiaos, who were only small-scale entrepreneurs, were unable
to finance such projects and had to sell out at below market rates. They
either went to Taiwan, emigrated to the United States, or moved to
other parts of Seoul (*The Economist*, 1986), thus contributing to the
disintegration of the Chinatowns.

There have been limits on the Huaqiaos' choice of occupation as
well. Engagement in international trade was restricted during the
1970s and '80s. Professions in government, law-related areas, and public school teaching were restricted [this is practiced by many countries,
including the United States]. Through restrictions on economic activities the Korean government limited the Huaqiaos' economic aspirations, causing students to migrate toward seemingly better opportunities in Taiwan. There also existed indirect discrimination against
Huaqiaos seeking employment opportunities. As a practice, most
Korean employers requested applicants to provide a census record,
which all Korean nationals have. The Huaqiaos, as foreign nationals
could not provide such a record, and were therefore, disqualified automatically from consideration for jobs.

In 1992, Korea and China normalized diplomatic relations; the result of Korea's interest in penetrating the Chinese market and China's desire to acquire Korean intermediary technologies. An increased demand soon followed for personnel who were fluent in both Korean and Chinese, especially those trained in Korean universities. The shift of Huaqiao students toward Korean universities coincided with this change in the international environment and the demand in the labor market.

Yet, the Huaqiaos contend, that in spite of the increased demand for their bilingual and bicultural skills, discrimination still persists. They insist that opportunities for promotion to decision-making executive levels are practically nil, and note that most of the Huaqiaos in Korean companies are lower-level clerks. Further, they view the Korean preference for inviting ethnic Koreans in China to Korea and/or employing them in mainland China (not to be mistaken with the Korean-Chinese (Huaqiaos) in Korea, whom I have been discussing) as a threat to Korean-Huaqiaos' new opportunities.

Chapter Six
Huaqiao Education in Korea

In his book, *Overseas Chinese Nationalism: The Genesis of the Pan-Chinese Movements in Indonesia, 1900-1916*, Lea Williams states that "Education . . . was the chief means for the national mobilization and the social, political, economic and psychological elevation of the Indies Chinese" (1960). This statement is useful in examining Korean-Huaqiaos' education.

Educational Policies

Ogbu (1988) asserts that minorities are found in "plural societies," societies with two or more populations within their respective political boundaries. A population within such a society or nation is a minority group, not because it is numerically smaller, but because it occupies a subordinate power position vis-à-vis another population within the same political boundary. This subordinate power position has important implications both for the way the minority group is treated in various domains of life, including education, and for the way the minority group members perceive and respond to events in those domains. Further, Ogbu observes that a minority population's view of schooling depends not only on how its members are treated by the dominant group, but also on the terms by which the society initially incorporated its minority population into its fold, such as whether the minorities joined the society more or less as voluntary immigrants or whether they were involuntarily bound to the society through slavery, conquest, or colonization. Ogbu's is an interesting framework by which to view Korean-Huaqiaos, whose status began as a voluntary minority but who were reduced to semi-involuntary status when they could not return to

their homeland. Further, the continuous deterioration of their economic status and their lack of political participation within the larger
Korean society resemble the characteristics of an involuntary minority.

Guskin (1968, p. 17) argues that education plays an important role
in assimilating immigrants into the host country, but then, at the same
time, it can play a direct role in maintaining ethnic identity. The
Chinese in Korea represent a classic example of the latter part of this
theory. Through their own separate education system that was sheltered from Korean influence, Korean-Huaqiaos maintained a greater
degree of ethnic identity. Further, this firm ethnic identity that was
sustained by language facility and a familiar educational system
induced Huaqiao students to select Taiwanese universities, a choice
that resulted in low morale for those Huaqiao students remaining in
Korea and maladjustment to their host country as a whole.

It is well established that high educational achievement is positive-
ly related to immigration. Thus, education not only influences the
choice of occupation but also social mobility. Rochey's (1976) study
showed that there is a high tendency for youth to seek alternate opportunities when society limits their occupational aspirations. I will examine Huaqiao education in Korea within the context of these frame-
works.

Korean policy for Huaqiao education is that of what Skinner
termed "ill-defined and *laissez faire*." Huaqiao schools in Korea are
unique because they exist outside the parameter of Korean educational law but they still function as schools. Huaqiaos in the past have
tended to deal with their own educational concerns without interference from the Korean government. Today, the district office sends out
a notification to the parents of Korean children when they reach school
age. The children of foreign nationals are eligible for Korean schools;
however, they are not required by the law to attend. Therefore, the district office does not send a notification to foreign children, a practice
that causes some misunderstanding and leads some Huaqiaos to
believe that Korean schools exclude them.

According to Korean law, all educational institutions are entitled to
certain benefits such as a reduction or an exemption from taxes.
However, Huaqiao schools are not entitled to such benefits as they are
not viewed as educational institutions by the Korean government. In
an interview, the principal of the Seoul Overseas Chinese High School
commented that Huaqiao school administrators are aware of these
financial benefits. However, they elect not to take advantage of them
because becoming a legal educational institution under Korean law
might subject them to Korean educational requirements, which could
hinder their students' ethnic education. Fees, donations, and occasional support from Taiwan largely operate the schools. The internal cul-

tures of the schools are identifiably Chinese, and the schools have retained strong links with the local Chinese community.

An interview with a law professor, he revealed that:

> Under Korean law Huaqiao schools are not a judicial body. Therefore, strictly speaking these schools are not schools. According to the law, they are just private organizations of foreign populations. Huaqiaos are operating them as schools, but they do not have any legal basis.

The Huaqiao situation contrasts with that of Malaysia, where Chinese education is a part of the national education system and is supported by the Malaysian government, and with that of Thailand and Indonesia, where the governments restrict ethnic education.

Significant historical developments help to clarify the relationship between Taiwan and the present-day Korean-Huaqiaos. The Overseas-Chinese were important to Taiwan in economic and political terms. Dr. Sun Yat-sen, the founder of the Republic of China (ROC) in 1911 on the mainland at the end of the Qing dynasty, solicited support from Overseas-Chinese communities. The 1911 Revolution, was partly financed by Overseas-Chinese. Dr. Sun's Nationalist Party (also referred as the Kuomintang or KMT), declared in 1929 that all Chinese, including the Overseas-Chinese, were Chinese nationals. The KMT, retreated to Taiwan under the leadership of Chang Kai-shek at the time of the Communist Revolution in China in 1949. KMT policy on Taiwan was, and still is aimed at securing the support and allegiance of the Chinese abroad. The Overseas-Chinese were encouraged to have a Chinese education and to orient themselves politically towards Taiwan. A number of seats in the Chinese (ROC) parliament were reserved for representatives of the Overseas-Chinese.

At present, there are twenty-eight elementary and four secondary Huaqiao schools, an extraordinary number of schools for such a small minority population. Most of these schools are equipped with dormitory facilities so they can be accessible to the Huaqiao children who are within commuting distance. As indicated earlier, some of these elementary schools are too small to be classified as a school and have only a handful of students. Often the school building consists of only one room without proper facilities. In some cases, when Huaqiao schools are not nearby in rural areas, Huaqiaos send their children to Korean schools, as do other Huaqiaos, citing the lack of academic standards at the ethnic schools. A few wealthy Huaqiaos, who appreciate English as a commercial language, send their children to American schools in Korea. However, these are exceptions, and in 1998 the total Huaqiao student population, those attending various schools and levels, was reported as

3,125, which is approximately sixteen percent of the total Huaqiao population. These figures testify to the popularity of the ethnic schools
among Huaqiao parents in Korea. The student population of these
schools varies greatly as some of the smallest regional schools have
fewer than ten students in the lower elementary level only and they
will be transferred to larger schools later on.

The Huaqiao schools are independent, and they follow the
Taiwanese curriculum and use *Guoyi*, Mandarin, as a medium of
instruction (Korea Huaqiaos Teachers Association, 1998). Some
Huaqiao parents whom I observed at the Seoul Overseas Elementary
School are strongly committed to the ethnic education of their children
and have made great sacrifices for their schooling. The School operates
a few mini-buses in the areas where the Huaqiao population is concentrated. However, the transportation service is not adequate to reach
the entire student population because the Huaqiaos are scattered
throughout Seoul. Therefore, many of the parents, especially those who
live far from the schools, assist in their children's commute. A school
administrator at the Seoul Overseas Chinese Elementary School estimates that approximately fifteen percent of elementary school students
were being assisted in commuting by their families. These family members, who are often mothers, are burdened financially and physically
because they must spend the entire day near their child's school. Most
of these parents are concerned about the quality of the school but reason that it is their ethnic duty to educate their children in Huaqiao
schools.

Recently in 1996, while the curriculum of most Huaqiao schools
remained unchanged, the Seoul Overseas Chinese High School adopted
Korean textbooks for their Korean university-bound students of the
eleventh and twelfth grades. Other schools and grades continue to use
Taiwan-supplied textbooks.

A teacher commented,

> Until now, we did not have enough foresight to provide an educa-
> tion which could be useful in Korean society. The Taiwanese system
> of education and the reality of Korean society are far apart. In the
> past, most went to Taiwan for higher education, but the trend is
> changing because of these new realizations.

Similar views of other Huaqiao community leaders could be summarized in this way by an interviewee:

> Huaqiao schools' curriculums are from Taiwan. Accordingly, if any-
> one wants to establish roots in Korea and live here, it [the curricu-
> lum] is inadequate. Not only must one know Korean history and

geography, but one must also know about Korean social reality and its judicial system, like their Korean peers.

Some of the recurring themes in interviews with community leaders, teachers, and parents include:

> The trend is changing now because it is not as easy to enter a Taiwanese university as before. Further, it is proven that Korean university graduates adjust better to life in Korea.

> Taiwan has changed a bit. In the past, after graduation from college we could easily remain in Taiwan and get a job. Now it has changed and one can no longer do that. You have to return to your place of residence for two years. There is a problem. When you return after two years, it is not easy to find a job. Korea has changed a lot also. Korea is under the management of the International Monetary Fund (IMF) now, but before the Korean economy was great. Business was doing well.

Mr. R attributes the maladjustment of the Huaqiaos in Korea to themselves as much as to the Korean government's policies. The Huaqiaos' pride in coming from the "middle kingdom," according to Mr. R, worked against them as they have not kept up with the changes in Korean society, and now, as a result, have became socially maladjusted and are losing the economic advantages they once enjoyed. Many second-generation interviewees, who are in their mid-40s and 50s, recalled that in the past Chinese parents did not allow them to play with Korean neighborhood kids due to Huaqiao parents' own ethnocentric attitudes, as described here.

The Huaqiao schools' education system, which differs from the Korean academic system, is a linear one of 6-3-3-4, consisting of six years of elementary school, three years of middle school, three years of high school, and four years of college. The academic year, modeled after the Taiwanese system, consists of two semesters. The first semester begins in September and ends in February, and the second semester runs from March to the end of July. Further, Huaqiao schools use textbooks provided by the Taiwanese government instead of Korean texts, and the majority of their teachers have been trained in Taiwan.

While most Huaqiaos express concern that their schools may not prepare their children academically, which may result in serious problems for the ethnic community in Korea, and, thus, require immediate reform, a few optimists predict that with the continuing prosperity of the Asian region the future of the Chinese schools looks incontestable among the Huaqiaos. The latter believe that the growing economic strength of China, especially, will enhance the social and economic value of the Chinese language and of an education in Chinese anywhere in Asia. Tan (1997) notes that in other countries, even in Singapore where the ethnic Chinese constitute more than seventy-five percent of the population, schools teaching entirely in Chinese no longer exist. In this sense, the Huaqiao schools in Korea are even more extraordinary.

The Taiwanese government's incentive policy of lower standards on entrance examinations, reduced tuition and dormitory costs, and special job placement after graduation, motivated many Huaqiao students in Korea to emigrate to Taiwan. This was an excellent opportunity for students who had been educated in Huaqiao schools that used a Taiwanese curriculum and textbooks, and who had received instruction in the Chinese language. Thus, students were well prepared to receive professional training at Taiwanese universities. Teachers in Huaqiao schools are usually Korean-Huaqiaos, who were trained at Taiwanese teachers' colleges.

Until recently, the development of the Chinese schools met with no interference but also no encouragement or support from the Korean government. The following comment by a Korean law professor reflects well the Korean attitude toward Huaqiao education.

> They [Huaqiaos] are not a threat to us [Koreans]. They are too few. There is no need to restrict their ethnic education and make them unhappy. Huaqiao education is o.k. as long as they are not teaching anti-Korean sentiment. Besides, we can benefit from bilingual and bicultural personnel, which Huaqiao schools produce.

Accordingly, the Korean government's position on education with respect to this minority population has been that of *laissez faire*, leaving the educational decisions of the ethnic minority up to the Chinese while heavily restricting other activities, especially in the economic arena. While the Huaqiao schools are not legally recognized as formal educational institutions, and thus exist solely as private organizations, the degrees conferred by these schools are recognized and they provide the graduates with the status of "study abroad" when they enter Korean universities.

The Korean system of accepting extra-quorum students at the university level is designed to attract foreign students and increase opportunities for the children of Korean expatriates to study in Korean universities. This law allows the president of each university to determine the qualifications of extra-quorum students. Although the original intention of this law was to attract the students who had graduated from secondary schools abroad, some universities extend this definition and include Huaqiao school graduates, allowing many Chinese students to choose most institutions of Korean higher education. Therefore, there is much variation in the interpretation of this law among universities. For example, Seoul National University maintains that a student must complete secondary school abroad in order to be eligible for admission. However, most private universities accept Huaqiao students if both parents are foreign nationals. Some of the less prestigious regional universities accept students as extra-quorum as long as the student is a foreign national. Strict interpretation of this regulation could jeopardize many students' academic careers. During the 1970s and 1980s a greater number of Koreans immigrated to the United States. At that time, many Korean youth who accompanied their parents returned to Korea for their higher education. This trend decreased when the immigrant population become mature and many members of the second generation became more familiar with English. The Huaqiaos' admission to Korean universities is in a way picking up the slack left by this decrease.

Still, the extra-quorum practice provides students the opportunity to enter Korean universities without much problem and with little academic preparation throughout high school. These seemingly advantageous Korean university admission policies work to the detriment of the Huaqiao students, however, as Huaqiao elementary and secondary schools continue to teach the Taiwanese curriculum and to neglect the teaching of the Korean language, Korean history, geography, and government, which students need for success in Korean universities. Inadequate preparation for a university education in Korea is thought to be the reason for the high attrition of Huaqiao students at these institutions (interview, August 1998).

Until 1996, Seoul Huaqiao High School had only one Korean teacher, who taught Physical Education, while the rest of the faculty was ethnic Chinese. With the increasing demand for Korean universities, newly appointed principal Sun, with the support of other faculty members, hired Korean teachers who had been educated in Korean universities to teach academic subjects for the Korean university track, making a landmark change. Since then, Principal Sun has been an advocate for Korean universities, arguing that the Huaqiaos must improve their lot in Korea and that Korean universities are the best means to this end. Following these initial changes, students' selection of Korean universities has steadily risen. At present, there are nineteen Korean university-educated Korean teachers and twenty-nine Taiwanese university-educated Huaqiao teachers on the faculty at the Seoul Overseas Chinese High School. SOCHS is the object of envy among other Huaqiao schools, because of the greater financial support it is receiving worked to its advantage. Other Huaqiao schools also recognize the need to change, but are unable to do so due to lack of resources. These schools claim that because of its location, SOCHS not only draws more students and local resources, but also greater attention from Taiwan.

Before 1953, teacher qualifications in Huaqiao schools varied. However, since 1954, the hiring of teachers has been limited to those who have passed the Taiwanese teacher certification examination. The graduates of Chinese schools in Korea were encouraged to attend teacher-training colleges in Taiwan. To accommodate the exploding school-age population of the Seoul Overseas High School, until 1974 there were elementary-level teacher training courses for those academically superior students interested in teaching. Upon graduation these students fulfilled the educational needs of the Huaqiao community. The Taiwanese government made additional arrangements for Huaqiao teachers from Korea to study in Taiwan in an attempt to improve the quality of Chinese education in Korea, and this practice still continues (personal communication, Aug. 1998).

With the increased number of teachers who have been educated in Taiwan, the Huaqiao schools' curriculum has been a replica of the Taiwanese educational system. As a consequence, while the high school course of study contained a stronger concentration of subjects such as Chinese, English, and mathematics, subjects like chemistry, physics, history, and geography received less emphasis. On the other hand, subjects such as the Korean language, Korean geography, and Korean history were neglected, with only three hours per week devoted to learning the Korean language, which is the minimum required by the Korean government (1975 school records). The weakness of this system is reflected in the experiences of the vast majority of Huaqiao students who entered Korean universities. Not only did many suffer from a lack of an academic vocabulary suitable for higher education, but many also recalled that they had difficulties because they did not have a knowledge of Korean geography and history, or simply general knowledge. Many of the Huaqiao students confessed that they are mostly engrossed with Huaqiao friends and schools, and that they were shocked by their poor academic background when they entered Korean universities.

My conversations with teachers at the Seoul Overseas Chinese Elementary School have confirmed that at the beginning of elementary school most Chinese students are more fluent in Korean. For some of the students, Korean is their only language; thus, the first couple of months of instruction must be carried on in Korean and Chinese, using Korean to explain the Chinese vocabulary the students are learning. By the third year, as students become comfortable in Chinese and later on gradually lose their Korean proficiency, they are strongly encouraged to speak only Chinese at school. Huaqiao youth are thus absorbed into the Chinese ethnic identity by the end of their secondary education.

Recently, the Korean-Huaqiao community experienced increased intermarriage between ethnic Chinese males and Korean females, with the result that many of their children are not familiar with the Chinese culture and language until they begin school. Huaqiao community leaders feel that their schools are important in order to instill ethnic pride and to transmit ethnic culture and language (interview, August 1998). In other words, the children's education plays a critical role in maintaining and intensifying their ethnicity.

As foreigners living in a foreign country where they are treated as aliens, the Korean-Huaqiaos are eager to establish at least a cultural link with the land of their origin. Therefore, Chinese schools in Korea are not commercial or profit-making ventures but rather public community projects. Money to keep the schools going is raised through annual donations, collection of monthly dues, and special fund-raising campaigns. Although the school board of trustees is elected, it is a self-perpetuating board, which re-elects its members from among themselves. The members are usually big financial contributors and community leaders. The situation for provincial schools is worse. Fewer students means less income from tuition fees, which also vary by area and grade. Most of the parents I have interviewed felt that the tuition was too high and that the schools lacked quality. Finally, since Taiwanese support is concentrated in Seoul Overseas Chinese Schools at all grade levels, other Huaqiao schools which constantly struggle to make ends meet.

Yet, the parents try their utmost into enroll their children in Huaqiao schools, not only for an ethnic education but also because the schools provide an easy avenue to higher education, as students are able to enter Taiwanese universities with lowered admission criteria and they have access to Korean universities, which take virtually all applicants. These options are not available for those Huaqiao students who study in Korean secondary schools, as they must take exams with Korean students to enter Korean universities, thus, ironically, penalizing Huaqiao students who studied in Korean schools. Also, the lack of Chinese language training when ethnic Chinese students attend Korean schools lessens their opportunity to study in Taiwanese universities. Strangely, Korean educational policy rewards those who study in ethnic schools.

In Chinese society, successful businessmen who aspire to be leaders will usually contribute handsomely to the welfare of their community. Making contributions to Huaqiao schools is an important part of such philanthropic activities and definitely enhances a man's social status. Thus, for wealthy Chinese, sitting on the boards of several organizations is one way of extending one's web of influence, patronage, and power. The broader function of the trustees is making major decisions regarding the direction of the school; the daily operation of school is left to the principal.

In the past, the trustees, made up mostly of businessmen who had received minimal education themselves, were not able to address the fundamental problems facing the schools. Therefore, these schools remained in many ways transplants of a system that had its origins in Taiwan but that was educating a generation of locally born children who were likely to continue living in Korea. Marilyn Clark (1965) in her book *Overseas Chinese Education in Indonesia* explains Chinese zeal in education in the following manner.

> It is a common generalization to ascribe to all Chinese an ethno-
> centric sense of superiority to other nations and peoples. To attrib-
> ute the parochial nature of the overseas Chinese to such chauvin-
> ism would be to oversimplify. If their aloofness can be partially
> explained by a sense of superiority, it is also to be remembered that
> most Chinese came to Indonesia as illiterate coolies and laborers
> with little awareness of traditional Chines culture. The Neo-
> Confucianism which spread among parts of the overseas Chinese
> community early in the 20th century, creating a desire for classical
> Chinese education, was actually reflective of a desire for the eleva-
> tion of status (Skinner, 1959, p. 3 quoted in Clark, 1965, p. 13).

Prior to Korean independence there existed very few historical records that can be studied to determine when and by whom ethnic Chinese schools were founded. The existence of these schools can be traced only through personal recollections. Chin (1979) recalls in his memoir that the earliest Chinese schools begun by the Huaqiao farmers in the Inchon area and the merchants' community schools in Pyungyang and Shinyijoo, present-day North Korea, were "community schools," where community members contributed by whatever means available to set up a school. These schools therefore, reflected the occupations of their founders. The erection of a Huaqiao school in 1902 in Inchon was rec-ognized as the first foreign school in Korea (Jeong, 1994), and it was patterned on a new concept of schooling: it had a proper building, trained teachers, regular timetables, and subjects such as history, geog-raphy, science, and physical education were introduced as part of the school curriculum (interview, 1999). In 1912, Seoul Overseas Chinese Elementary School was established (Seoul Overseas Chinese High School year book, 1998).

However, Chinese schools in Korea existed before the above men-tioned modern schools and these schools were replicas of old style *sishu* - private schools.

Sishu, a type of one-teacher private school, was the primary form for teaching literacy and preparing scholars for the imperial examination. Students were taught individually or in groups, with the teacher being hired by individual families or a village, or operating the school himself. Teachers relied on fees and tuition for survival, and some simply ate or lived in a student's home. Textbooks were classical cannons that embodied moral teaching and scientific and commonsense knowledge. Rote learning was universally adopted, and corporal punishment was not only accepted but encouraged. Sishu continued to operate in China's vast rural areas until 1949, when the People's Republic of China was established (Lin, 1999, p. 4).

In Qing China there was a broad demand for basic or elementary education which was provided through the family or through the neighborhood schools organized at the local level. Korean-Huaqiaos brought the teachers from China and the curriculum included "the use of the abacus, rote-learning of the 'Four Books' (*Analects, The Doctrine of the Mean, The Great Learning,* and *Mencius*), and how to write a conventional letter" (Purcell 1951 quoted in Clark 1965, p. 18). Through these three texts, a student could learn up to 2,000 Chinese characters as well as acquire a smattering of history and traditional ethics.

However, Lin notes change occurred as the political situation in China changed.

After the Opium war in the 1840s, national defeat and humiliation caused reformers in China to call for educational development, which was deemed to be vital for the survival and strengthening of the country. Conscientious intellectuals and citizens demanded the abolition of the imperial examination system and the popularization of education. "New learning" was prescribed as the panacea to cure the ills of the traditional teaching of classical canons, which turned out "bookworms" good only at taking examinations. Many schools were set up, including general primary and secondary schools for boys and girls, vocational technical schools, military and marine training schools, commerce schools, and liberal arts schools. They appeared to spread literacy and teach Western science and technology (Lin, 1999, p. 4)

Although the Inchon Huaqiao school in 1912 is recorded as the first foreign school in Korea, it was only for an elite few and the vast majority of ethnic Chinese in Korea were educated in *sishu* type of schools, learning some rudimentary literacy and numeracy skills. During the

Korean War (1950-1953), Huaqiao education was held in the Taiwanese Legation (it was called the Chinese Legation at that time for the South Korean government was at war with the People's Republic of China and recognized the Republic of China, Taiwan, as the only legitimate government of China) compound at Pusan, the refugee capital of war-time Korea. Only after the Korean War did modern schools, replicating the Taiwanese system, became popular.

Throughout the Japanese colonial period in Korea (1910-1945), the Chinese schools in Korea were directly under the jurisdiction of the Japanese colonial government, which represented an enemy state. Adequate educational provisions were made for the children of Japanese expatriates only, and the elite sent their children to Japan for further education, while educational opportunity for Korean youth was severely limited. Moreover, the establishment of schools was restricted, the use of Korean as a medium of instruction was prohibited, and the teaching of Korean history was prohibited. In addition, communicating in Korean was forbidden according to a Japanese policy to *"Nipponize"* the local population. These policies applied to Huaqiao schools in Korea. Due to such severe restrictions, only a few elementary schools were added during this time.

Following Korean independence in 1945 and the establishment of the Republic of Korean in 1948, an educational law was enacted. A compulsory education system was introduced and adopted as the 6-3-3-4 linear school system. Both adult education, to eliminate illiteracy, and supplementary in-service education for teachers were introduced. Expansion planning for secondary and higher education and the creation of teachers colleges developed during this period.

During the post-war era, the Korean government was overwhelmed by the educational needs of its own people. New insistent demands for education on the part of the Koreans absorbed the greater part of the available resources. The Huaqiaos, left largely to their own devices, financed further rapid expansion of schools for their own children. The demand for schooling among the Huaqiaos continued unabated for the next decade. The number of elementary schools reached fourteen and the student population grew to 2,000, which was approximately ten percent of the total Huaqiao population in Korea (Park, 1986). After the Korean War, the Huaqiao schools were reconstructed and reestablished with the help of the Chinese Embassy (then Taiwan). By 1957, there were thirty-six elementary schools and three middle schools. Seoul Overseas Middle School was set up, and it graduated eighteen students in 1955. Due to the difficulty of students going to Taiwan for high school, a high school was organized in Seoul and produced its first ten graduates in 1958 (Seoul Overseas Chinese High School Brochure, 1998).

The most notable feature of the 1950s through the 1970s is the growth of Korean-Huaqiaos' secondary education. By 1974, the numbers rose to fifty elementary schools and five secondary schools. The impetus for this expansion of Huaqiao schools came from two social forces: a rapidly expanding population, with increasing numbers of children reaching school age, and a surge in the demand for education, which had come to be perceived as essential to social advancement. Several factors contributed to this growth. Some of the demand came from the young Huaqiaos, whose educational opportunities had been limited by Japanese colonial rule and interrupted by the subsequent Korean War. Increases in primary school enrollments further added to the numbers seeking secondary education. While before the war it was possible to send older children to China to continue their schooling, this option was no longer available after the Communist victory in 1949. Thus, there was a greater demand for secondary education to be available locally. Finally, the increased need for secondary education was part of a change in attitude toward education, for interest in education rose as more and more people came to realize its value as the key to advancement in life. Education, in other words, was desired for its economic value.

After the Korean War, the student enrollment in ethnic schools reflected trends among the Huaqiao population in Korea (see figure 3).

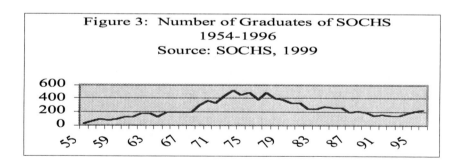

Figure 3: Number of Graduates of SOCHS
1954-1996
Source: SOCHS, 1999

At this time, the Huaqiao population increase was due to a higher birth rate, since no more new immigrants were arriving from mainland China. Chinese immigration was curved, first, due to the severing of the diplomatic ties between the mainland China and South Korea and the prohibition of contact between the two countries and, second, because of the South Korean government's immigration restrictions, which were intended to protect Korea as it was suffering from a population explosion. This natural increase of the Chinese population continued until the early 1970s. It can be surmised that during this time the rise in population was predominantly due to the marriage of ethnic Chinese men and Korean women, as the ethnic Chinese population was largely male prior to this time, and the Korean War had prevented Chinese from returning to China. Through these new unions, the number of Chinese children born in Korea increased after the Korean War, and the Chinese community became permanently settled in Korea. This natural increase of the Chinese population continued until the early 1970s.

1976 saw the greatest number of ethnic Chinese high school students graduate, with 440 students receiving their diplomas from the Seoul Overseas Chinese High School. After 1976, the student population began to decrease and continued throughout the '80s.

According to an alumnus of SOCHS,

> I graduated from the Seoul Overseas Chinese High School in 1972 and went to Taiwan. The majority of the students at that time went to Taiwanese universities, well over half, and I think it may have been about two-thirds. Some went to Korean universities. Some went to the United States or Australia for study. Most of my high school friends reside in the United States. Many of those who studied in Taiwan went to the United States for a Master's and so on. The next choice is Taiwan, with the fewest alumni residing in Korea.

While many of those who studied in Taiwan stayed there, others utilized Taiwanese universities as an initial route to emigrate elsewhere, such as to the United States or Australia.

Another element is that institutional accommodations made available to Huaqiao students by the Taiwanese government encouraged these students. The following statement by an interviewee summarizes:

> During the '70s, there were lots of benefits provided by the Taiwanese government for those students who were entering Taiwanese universities, such as tuition assistance, subsidized dormitory expenses, health insurance, etc. . . . It was cheaper to go to Taiwan than to study in Korea . . . while the academic standing of Taiwanese universities was higher than that of Korean universities. Also, we were treated well in Taiwanese universities. In

Taiwan, each university president assumed the role of guardian and was responsible for our welfare. When we had a problem we could seek help from the president of the school we were attending. The presidents then requested the cooperation of the faculty and so on.

During the 1970s and 1980s, education played an important role in the emigration of the ethnic Chinese from Korea, who often used Taiwan as a stepping stone to move elsewhere. Another interviewee commented,

Not all of them stayed in Taiwan. . . . Back then, many Korean-Huaqiao students went to the United States for study after graduating from Taiwanese universities, planning to settle down later on. There are many Korean-Huaqiaos in America. I am also a permanent resident of the United States. Every time I visit the United States or Taiwan I bump into many familiar faces.

Many others echoed this interviewee's comments about immigration opportunities.

Most of my alumni friends are in the United States and Taiwan . . . . especially most of my female alumnae friends are in Taiwan.

Since 1974, as the ethnic Chinese have emigrated to Taiwan, the United States, and other countries, the number of students and schools in Korea has declined. By 1979, there were only thirty-nine Chinese elementary schools and five high schools in Korea. Presently, there are twenty-eight elementary schools and four high schools, with the Seoul Overseas Chinese Schools, both elementary and secondary, having the greatest number of students.

The emigration of Huaqiao youth, especially the females, influenced the social dynamic of this minority group, a phenomenon mirrored in increased intermarriages between Koreans and Huaqiaos. According to a Seoul Overseas Elementary School teacher, her school has had steady increase of students from mixed backgrounds.

Students with Korean mothers are increasing, and approximately 30-40 percent of the entering students' mothers are Koreans. Last year was the highest with fifty-two percent. This year I have not tallied yet, but I suspect the figure will remain high.

Mr. Z, one of the interviewees, who is also married to a Korean, explained the rise in interethnic marriage in this way.

> We [Korean-Chinese students] were not studious, and we barely passed. Girls saw no future from us but managing Chinese restaurants so they left for Taiwan. Both parents wanted to send their children away, and the children wanted to get away. There weren't that many marriageable Huaqiao females in Korea. Most of my high school alumni friends, I think seventy to eighty percent, married Korean women.

Mr. Z sees many faults in the older generation, who failed to provide younger generations with the values necessary for living in Korea. He said the "older generation Huaqiaos constantly complain about Korean society but their failure to take action to improve their situation made the young generations feel helpless."

> Younger Korean women who are married to Huaqiaos are different than their older generation counterparts, who married Huaqiao men and learned the Chinese language and culture. According to Chinese community leaders, "although they send their children to Huaqiao schools, these young Koreans are not willing to learn Chinese and insist upon Korean language and customs. Consequently, the home language and culture are more exclusively Korean."

Teaching in Huaqiao schools has been affected by the increasing number of children who come to school without any knowledge of Chinese. Ms. H explains the strategy of teaching Chinese in the elementary grades this way:

> The opportunity to speak Chinese [at home] is minimal for most of the students. So in my instruction for first grade, I have to speak both languages for the first couple of months. I have to speak in Korean and repeat in Chinese. Sometimes I have to say something twice in Korean. When I explain vocabulary, it is easier for students to understand in Korean than if I explain in Chinese. After a couple of months I reduce the use of Korean, but I do not prohibit the use of it. If I do so, then the children will not come to me. I just lead them to speak Chinese within the vocabularies that they have learned. So, in the first grade both Chinese and Korean are spoken. By the second semester it is much easier to conduct a lesson. Some of the third grade teachers restrict students from speaking Korean, but I do not know how well the students grasp the Chinese.

Many Huaqiao leaders are concerned that if this trend continues, Huaqiaos in Korea will be absorbed into Korean society and will disappear. Others agree with Mr. S and add that whole social environment, especially the influence of TV, is heading in this direction. Some young Huaqiao parents who are second or third generation are comfortable in Korean, and Korean has become the home language, even though both parents are Huaqiao. One of the interviewees explained the difficulty of maintaining the use of Chinese at home.

> My husband and I both are Huaqiao but we speak Korean at home. You see, both of us are working, so most often we only get to see our children before their bedtime. It is very difficult to teach Chinese then, and to explain everything in Chinese to our children, who have Korean friends and watch Korean TV all day long.

Many Huaqiao males who are married to Korean women, including Mr. Z, see more benefits in assimilating their children into the Korean culture and language since they are living in Korea. Ironically, the more intermarriage occurs, the more the Huaqiaos resoundingly express a greater need for ethnic education, as schools are the last place where their ethnic heritage can be preserved.

Since 1945, the Huaqiao schools in Korea have changed very little. The textbooks for these schools are still supplied by the Taiwanese government, which continues to aid in teacher training. By means of textbooks and teachers, the Chinese schools continue to foster a Taiwanese orientation among Huaqiao students. Since no textbooks are used that present a Korean perspective, students become familiar with Taiwan and learn little or nothing about their host country. A community leader confided,

> I am very ashamed of the fact that there is no vision in the Chinese community regarding the education of Huaqiao youth. Since 1992, the Chinese community has been experiencing a setback, and the Huaqiao community is not coping well with these changes. We are in a transitional period, but the Chinese community is not coming up with any solutions to address this change. In the past, the Taiwanese government in every respect supported us, including educational matters. We had easier placement in a university, although we were not exempted from exams. Since 1992, we have been experiencing a changed attitude and policy on the part of the Taiwan government. They [Taiwanese government] treat us [Huaqiaos] more like foreigners now.

The Huaqiaos call the 1990s a "transitional period." Much has changed in Korea, and the Huaqiaos are trying to adapt to the changes. Since the late 1980s, there has been an increasing demand for Korean universities among Huaqiao youth, and emigration to Taiwan by way of Taiwanese universities seems to have ceased. Some Huaqiaos even suggest that there has been a trend of reverse immigration to Korea by their people, who left during the 1980s, and they concede that in many respects, such as the economy and social opportunities, the situation in Korea is better than in previous decades.

Chapter Seven

Gender and Ethnicity in College Choices

Featherman and Hauser's (1978) analysis leads us to conclude that education has been an avenue of occupational attainment for immigrant groups. High educational attainment has facilitated the mobility of some immigrant groups, while lack of schooling has severely impeded the ability of other groups to move up the ranks occupationally. However, the literature indicates a persuasive coalition between general attitudes of a given minority community and individual choice. For example, in the United States, both foreign-born and second-generation Mexican men suffer an occupational disadvantage due to their low levels of education while Russian Jews have achieved greater occupational status by attaining higher levels of education (Olneck, 1995). Examining data from the 1976 Survey of Education and Income, Hirschman and Wong (1984) found similar results, and concluded that "It is only through overachievement in education that Asian-Americans reach socioeconomic parity with the majority population"(p. 600).

Nevertheless, in a different context, Korean-Huaqiaos' educational choices led to a lowered occupational status for them in Korea. Due to the Huaqiaos schools' adoption of a Taiwanese curriculum that did not coincide with the Korean situation, and to the development of a leadership vacuum for those remaining in Korea, the ethnic Chinese failed to adjust to the larger society. The Korean-Huaqiaos' presence in Taiwanese institutions of higher education was ranked third in absolute numbers and first in proportion to its population. Korean-Huaqiao graduates of Taiwanese universities recount that peer pressure, the curriculum, and the prospect of better job opportunities upon graduation influenced their decision to attend college in Taiwan. These choices led to the decrease of the Huaqiao population in Korea, which in turn influenced the social dynamics within the Korean-Huaqiao community.

The Huaqiao community's focus on Taiwanese universities has had serious educational and social implications for this ethnic minority. However, the trend in the 1990s appears to be the reverse of that of the 1970s and 1980s in that Huaqiao students now predominately favor Korean universities. This shift in educational choice from Taiwanese to Korean universities was brought about by various influences, including social changes within the Korean and the Huaqiao societies and also broader economic and political currents. The recent move toward Korean universities by Huaqiao students may reflect their elevated opportunities in the dominant society.

Korean-Huaqiao Students in Taiwanese Universities

Gibson (1991) asserted that schools in America are of crucial significance in conditioning the encounter between immigrant communities and America. Immigrants tend to regard schools, despite the cultural threats they pose, as welcome avenues to participation and mobility (Caplan et al., 1991; Delgado-Gaitan and Trueba, 1991; Suarez-Orozco, 1991; Matute-Bianchi, 1991). Tyack (1974) summarized the dual nature of Americanization by observing that it cultivated both modern habits and Anglo-conformity, and that it promoted both equal opportunity and social control. Dash Moore (1981) has found that New York's second-generation Jewish immigrant adults, having attained the political power associated with middle-class status, pressured the schools to recognize and accommodate Jewish ethnicity, most prominently by including Hebrew as a foreign language in the high schools, and by accommodating the schools' calendars to the demands of Jewish observances. Attainment of the political capacity to press ethnic demands, albeit modest ones, rather than intergenerational change in ethos away from assimilation and toward pluralism, accounts for this shift (Olneck, 1995).

Unlike the heterogeneous American model, Korea is an extremely homogeneous society where a high degree of social cohesion exists. Thus, since there is little need for Korea to impose cultural and linguistic adaptation on its ethnic minority, the larger society can allow operation of a separate school system. While ethnic education enhances ethnic identity and maintains Chinese cultural heritage, the minority population has been inefficient in adapting to the broader society, resulting in a lack of social/occupational mobility for its members.

Many studies concluded that immigrant belief in, and dependence on the efficacy of schooling is not a fixed article of faith that is unresponsive to objective realities and to shifts in a group's perception of its status and opportunities (Gibson & Bhachu, 1991; Matute-Bianchi, 1991). The Korean-Huaqiaos' recent preference for Korean universities fits into this framework, which has changed over time according to how they have viewed the opportunities available to them.

According to statistics from the Overseas Chinese Affairs Commission (1999), 66,059 Overseas-Chinese students graduated from Taiwanese higher education institutions from 1952 to 1995. Korean-Huaqiao students represent twelve percent of the total graduating Overseas-Chinese, following Hong Kong/Macao (thirty-five percent) and Malaysia (twenty-nine percent). Korea's representation surpasses that of Indonesia (7.5 percent), Vietnam (5.5 percent), Burma (4.9 percent), Thailand (2.6 percent), Singapore (one percent), the Philippines (0.7 percent), and Japan (O.6 percent). It is estimated that there are approximately fifty-five million Overseas-Chinese, and that about eighty percent of them reside in Southeast Asian countries: six million in Hong Kong, half a million in Macao, five million in Malaysia, over seven million in Indonesia, 8.5 million in Thailand, 2.7 million in Singapore, and 2.3 million in Vietnam (*http://www.odci.gov/cia/publications/factbook*, 1999). Considering that there are only some 20,000 Huaqiaos in Korea, the absolute numbers and the proportion of Korean-Huaqiaos students in the Taiwanese higher education system is astonishing when compared to the ratio of the Huaqiao population of each country, the Korean-Huaqiaos' participation in Taiwanese higher education easily ranks first. These statistics lead to the conclusion that in the past, the Korean-Huaqiaos saw their opportunities in Taiwan, not in Korea.

Trends in the Selection of Higher Education Among Korean-Chinese Students

In this section, looking at the trend of higher education selection will give us a broader picture of the perceived economic and political realities of the Korean-Huaqiaos. According to data from the Overseas-Chinese Commission (1998), which is a cabinet level ministry in Taiwan, the first four Korean-Huaqiao students graduated from Taiwanese postsecondary educational institutions in 1953. Five years later, in 1958, twenty-seven Huaqiao students, a 575 percent increase from 1953, graduated from Taiwanese institutions. In 1960, statistics show a 189 percent increase from 1955; in 1965 there was an eighty-five percent increase from 1960; in 1970 there was a seventy-five percent increase from 1965; in 1975 there was a ninety percent increase from 1970; and in 1980, there was a fifty-three percent increase. These are phenomenal increases when compared to the initial year of 1953. Yet, only a three percent increase occurred between 1980 and 1985. During the 1970s and the early 1980s, Korea was not economically and political-ly stable; therefore, it could not provide equitable policies for all those who reside within its boundaries. The first year of continuous decrease began in 1986, with a seven percent decrease from the previous year. The decrease of 1986 was followed by a twenty percent decrease in 1987, a thirty-six percent decrease in 1988, an eight percent decrease in 1989, and a fifteen percent decrease in 1990. Throughout the 1990s there was a steady decrease: a twenty-nine percent decrease in 1991, a forty-nine percent decrease in 1992, a fifty-one percent decrease in 1993, a ninety-two percent decrease in 1994, and a sixty-nine percent decrease in 1995. The Korean-Huaqiaos' caravan destined for Taiwan began in the late 1960s and peaked during the 1970s and early 1980. The change in the trend in the late 1980s and 1990s is significant as it coincides with the economic development and political stabilization in Korea, which infers that a parallel exists between economic opportunity and school choices. Not only do the Korean-Huaqiaos see more economic opportunities but the new generation of Huaqiaos may feel more comfortable with Korean culture. While an element of discrimination may still exist, Korean soci-ety, which has became more confident with its national identity, econom-ic achievement, and political stability might also now be more open and willing to embrace its minority population.

Noting that about two-thirds of Huaqiao students during the 1970s went to Taiwanese universities, many of the interviewees conceded that academic prestige among their peers, and limited social and eco-nomic mobility in Korea led them to Taiwanese universities. Mr. H's following explanation, echoed by many, adds a dimension of under-standing to the relationship between perceived opportunity, peer pres-sure, and educational background and college choice.

> Back in the 1970s, the trend was that academically able students went to Taiwanese universities and less able students went to Korean universities. So, going to Taiwan was seen as success. It has lot to do with the occupational opportunities of the Huaqiaos in Korea. Korean-Huaqiaos at that time were, and still are, mostly engaged in Chinese restaurants and young Huaqiaos despised it. The Taiwanese economy was fast-growing then, and it was very easy to find a job [in Taiwan] upon college graduation.

The possibility to get out from food industry through Taiwanese uni-versities was an attractive option to many Korean-Huaqiao youth who were suffering from economic and occupational deprivation in Korea while the easier admission made available to Huaqiao students by Korean universities lowered the prestige of Korean universities as a whole.

On the other hand, an interviewee claimed that for many Huaqiaos during the 1970s, Korean universities were "remote." This informant claimed that not only ethnocentric attitudes and dim occupational prospects for the future forced them into Taiwanese universities, but also that the Huaqiaos were not familiar with the admission process of Korean universities. He believed that during that time few Huaqiaos with "connections" to Korean universities went to Korean universities, which sounds like a contradiction of his and others' statements.

Many Huaqiaos educated in Taiwanese universities claimed that Korean universities' tuition was out of reach for them, in addition to the grim occupational possibilities in Korea. However, other Korean university-educated Huaqiaos claimed they chose these institutions, because of financial reasons. Admitting that Korean universities' tuition was higher than that of Taiwanese universities' subsidized rate for Huaqiaos, one interviewee explained:

> I chose a Korean university because our family could not afford to send me to a Taiwanese university. My family operated a small Chinese restaurant in Daegu, and it was difficult for them to come up with the large amount of deposit of 6 months living expenses in Taiwan. Attending a Korean university relieved such pressure as I was supplied with *Hyangto janghakkum* (a hometown scholarship, student slang for money sent from home) as the need arose.

Several other Korean university graduates indicated in interviews that they chose Korean universities because they had to work to support themselves through college. These interviews therefore, provide an allowance to deduce that a greater number of those who went to Taiwanese universities were middle class Huaqiaos than those who went to Korean universities, while those who attended Korean universities are either the most affluent, thus having more connection to and more stake in Korean society, or poor families who could not afford to send them to Taiwan. Another Korean university-educated Huaqiao said that he was given a full scholarship throughout his academic career study by winning a "Korean Language Speech Contest for Foreigners." Moreover, other interviewees who graduated from Korean universities added that partial scholarships were available to them from each university. Therefore, it is possible that those students who went to Taiwanese universities may have been less well connected to Korean society, and thus, experienced a lack of information, possibly resulting from lack of interest.

Many of those who studied in Taiwan during the 1970s disclosed that they never considered studying at a Korean university, stating that the Huaqiao schools' Taiwanese-style curriculum played a critical role in their selection of a Taiwanese university. Mr. H's following explanation was resoundingly reported by others who studied in Taiwanese universities.

> It was natural for me to choose a Taiwanese university since I followed the Taiwanese curriculum throughout my schooling. Most students went to Taiwan because it was more popular and easier to study as we had studied the Taiwanese way.

Since the 1980s, the Huaqiao students' preoccupation with Taiwan seems to have cooled down. Interviews reveal that during the 1970s, however, going to Taiwanese universities upon graduation from Huaqiao high schools was trendy, and that it provided academic prestige among peers because entrance to these universities required more rigorous preparation than admission to Korean universities. Interestingly, the easier admission made available to Huaqiao students by Korean universities lowered the prestige of Korean universities as a whole. To many Huaqiao students, going to Taiwanese universities was synonymous with success. According to an interviewee:

> It was popular to go to Taiwan then [in the 1970s], and I went along with this mood. During my day, upon Huaqiao school graduation, only students with good academic standing were given the privilege of taking the exam for Taiwanese universities. That privilege was granted by the Taiwanese Ministry of Education.

Another interviewee narrated the following:

> Back in the 1970s, the trend was that [the most] academically qualified students went to Taiwanese universities and less qualified students went to Korean universities.

Without exception, all graduates recalled the popularity of the Taiwanese university track:

> When I was in SOCHS [graduated in 1973], there were seven classes. One class consisted of 50 to 60 students. So, each grade had approximately 350 students. I was from the baby boomer generation after the Korean War, and the classrooms were crowded. Of the seven classes, one class was for those who were applying to Korean universities. The rest were the Taiwanese university track, and each student selected his or her track.

Therefore, multiple forces pushed Huaqiaos toward Taiwanese universities: a strong ethnic identity instilled through ethnic education, economic incentives, peer pressure, and, most of all, language ability, which enabled students to integrate themselves into Taiwanese universities. Second-generation Huaqiaos had a stronger ethnic identity that came directly from being raised by first-generation immigrants. Further, these younger people had better Chinese language proficiency as they had communicated with first-generation immigrants who are usually less competent in Korean.

Interviewees elucidated that the Taiwanese curriculum they studied and peer pressure were catalysts for going to Taiwan. The following views were widely shared by those who went to Taiwanese universities:

> It was natural for me to choose a Taiwanese university since I was educated with a Taiwanese curriculum throughout my entire school career.

Another recalled:

> Most students went to Taiwan because it was popular and easier because we studied that [Taiwanese] way.

Another added:

> It has a lot to do with the education we had received so far. We had been receiving the Taiwanese style of education, and it was easier that way [study in Taiwan].

The Taiwanese education the Huaqiaos received contributed to the patriotic feelings of these expatriates:

> I think for most of us China [the mainland] is our [ancestral] home but Taiwan is our motherland. This is because we are nourished by Taiwanese education.

For many Korean-Huaqiaos, Taiwan represented China, and returning to Taiwan symbolized returning to Chinese roots. But later, in the 1990s, when the Taiwanese became more politically and culturally assertive about distinguishing their separate heritage from that of mainland China, the Korean-Huaqiaos, who were ancestrally and thus culturally tied to mainland China, began to feel more left out. Many interviewees expressed that Taiwan no longer seemed like "China" to them. With the reestablishment of diplomatic relations between Korea and China, the Korean-Huaqiaos could now go to the "real" China thus, need for substitution diminished.

College Choices and the Effects on the Huaqiao Population

The impact of the Huaqiaos' choice of Taiwanese universities was immediately felt in their ethnic community, which experienced a population decrease, but there was also a long-term, more complicated effect. Because going to Taiwan was regarded as a sign of success, feelings of inadequacy prevailed among those who remained in Korea and made them feel excluded from opportunities for greater economic and social mobility. Another issue was that educational choices led to a gender imbalance, which in turn caused a different marriage and family pattern among the Huaqiaos. The resulting diluted ethnic identity among members of the younger generation led them to choose a different educational path today.

Ethnic Identity and College Choice

Very little research has been done in Korea regarding the Korean-Huaqiaos. It is clear, however, that Chinese in Korea share the same place of origin and language; through kinship relations, they have also maintained a great degree of cohesion. Further, common experience as a minority population in Korea has forged a keen bond of ethnic identity.

Gosling (1983) classifies four types of adaptation models used by the ethnic Chinese in Southeast Asian countries: The earliest and continuing influence is toward adaptation, accommodation, and even assimilation into local societies and cultures; a second shift, which has become more powerful in recent decades, has been reemphasis on or in some cases the rise of a common Chinese culture; a third shift has been towards a Western model, first a colonial and now a universal modern model; a fourth shift in identity, often prevented or obscured by the previous shifts, is the movement from ethnic identity towards class-based identity.

In August 1998, a survey question, "How do you describe yourself best?" was asked of 140 ethnic Chinese students who were then attending the Seoul Overseas Chinese High School in Seoul, Korea. I chose this population because over sixty percent of the Korean-Chinese reside in Seoul, and this is the largest Chinese secondary school in Korea, enrolling two-thirds of the total ethnic Chinese high school population. Also, its student body comes from various areas of Korea. In this survey, eighty-six percent of the students identified themselves as Chinese who live in Korea (Korean-Chinese or Korean-Huaqiao), ten percent as

Chinese, three percent as Koreans of Chinese extraction, and only one
percent as Korean (see table 2).

Table 2: Self-Described Identity of SOCHS Seniors, 1999		
		N = 134
Identity	Frequency	(Percent)
Chinese	14	(10.4)
Chinese who live in Korea (Korean-Huaqiao)	115	(85.8)
Korean with Chinese Ancestry (*Huaren*)	4	(3.0)
Korean	1	(0.7)

These responses appeared to reflect the patrilineal legal characteristics
of East Asian countries, i.e. an individual is automatically given citizenship if his/her father is a citizen. Thus, most of the respondents,
who were born and raised in Korea, have not lived in or traveled to
China, the country of their ancestral origins, nor to Taiwan, the country of their citizenship. Recently these countries are moving away from
patrilineal practices and toward granting citizenship to children of
mixed union, regardless of a parent's gender.

A second survey was conducted in June 1999 with the same population to get more insight into their responses. In addition to the first
survey question, "How do you best describe yourself?" this survey
urged students to describe the reason(s) for their response by asking
"Why do you feel that way?" to which they responded in essay form.
This survey showed marked differences from the previous survey.
Seventy-four percent of the students identified themselves as Korean-
Chinese, fifteen percent as Korean with Chinese ancestry, nine percent
as Chinese, and two percent as Korean, revealing the fluidity of ethnic
identity. Huaqiao youths' responses to the question, "Why do you feel
that way?" were more revealing than the statistics of the surveys, and
revealed some differences between Korean university-track students
and Taiwanese university-track students in their professed identities.
While the number of students who identified themselves as Koreans of
Chinese ancestry in the Korean university track was greater than in
the Taiwanese track, the number of students who identified themselves
as Chinese was greater in the Taiwanese than in the Korean university track, suggesting the influence of ethnic identity in college choice
among the Chinese in Korea. The more strongly one affiliates with
Chinese ethnic identity, the greater the chance that he/she will seek
education in Taiwan; one who identifies more with the Korean culture
and language will likely choose a Korean university.

Further, Korean university-track students displayed more complexity in their identity by adding their "cultural/linguistic" identity in varying degrees, but they unfailingly emphasized their similarity with Koreans, especially in terms of language and culture. According to a respondent, "My Taiwanese nationality is the only reminder that I am not a Korean, otherwise I am like any other Korean." Many others expressed similar sentiments. Another student articulated,

> I am a fourth generation Korean-Chinese. I was born and raised in Korea [and my parents also]. I am more comfortable with the Korean language and culture than Chinese. In fact, I think I am more Korean than Chinese. I am Chinese in nationality but Korean in reality.

For these students, China is a rather remote land of their ancestors' and their past while Korea is their present and future. A few of them indicated an interest in visiting China and possibly of doing business in the future, yet none indicated an interest in making China their home, asserting that their stakes are in Korea, not China, where their immediate ancestors came from.

> Ethnically I am full-blooded Chinese. But it is very difficult to call myself Chinese since I am very *Koreanized*. I often think about my country [China]. But I think I would be a stranger there.

A few students who had the opportunity to visit mainland China and/or Taiwan demonstrated similar apprehensions:

> I visited Taiwan and China on a few occasions but I felt I was a stranger in either place. I have difficulties with Chinese food and even the language. I am not an authentic Chinese but a Korean-Huaqiao.

Another student reported:

> Once I visited China and I had a very difficult time with the language and food. I was so glad to be back [in Korea]. One week in China was plenty for me.

For these students, the lack of Korean citizenship rather than Chinese ethnicity was the psychological barrier to being fully Korean:

> I consider myself more Korean than Chinese, but I am not a Korean citizen. I do not carry a census card like Koreans. Instead I carry a resident alien card for foreign nationals.

Many other students echoed this sentiment. While these students identify themselves as Koreans culturally and their families have lived in Korea for generations, as foreign nationals they must get permission to reside in Korea, which must be renewed every five years (formerly every two years). Further, when they travel abroad they must apply for reentry to come home, a requirement which according to them, "is a reminder that they are not Koreans."

The issue of ethnic identity is more complicated for the students of a mixed background. Unlike in the past, an increasing number of individuals from mixed ethnic backgrounds now question the laws which assign their ethnic boundaries according to patriarchal practice. An interviewee claimed that,

> Ethnically and culturally I am more Korean than Chinese but my nationality is Taiwan. My grandfather [father's side] escaped from China and married my grandmother, who is a Korean. My mother is Korean, which makes me three-fourths Korean and only one-fourth Chinese. Culturally, we are completely Korean. Speaking Korean, eating Korean food, etc.

The words of these interviewees imply that the denial of citizenship based on the paternal line is legal hogwash. For these students, both Taiwan and China are ethnically and emotionally remote lands, and they express the hope of Chinese and Koreans working together toward positive inter-group relations.

On the other hand, the majority of Taiwanese university-track students claimed roots, blood, and Chinese heritage as the basis for their identity; therefore, they demonstrated a highly salient ethnicity and a degree of ethnocentric attitudes. Further, this group of students reported that they have not given any thought to independent or individual identity, and that they accept the ascribed Korean-Huaqiao identity more readily than do their Korean university-track counterparts.

Naturally, there was a difference in each group's attitude towards college choices. While Korean university-track students viewed Korean universities as a vehicle to adapt to Korean society by achieving socialization through the Korean system and people as preparation for living in Korea, Taiwanese university-track students emphasized their ethnic identity by reflecting in their college choice - the desire to "learn more about the Chinese language and culture" in order to become "proper Chinese." Further, some of these students expressed the desire to relocate to Taiwan as a reason for their college choice. One of these students exhibited ethnic pride in the following way: "Historically, China had a greater civilization, and at present Taiwan has a higher standard of living." Concerned about the present status of the Korean economy, some students thought that in Taiwan "it will be easier to get a job," or that the twenty-first century will be the "golden age for China," and studying in a Taiwanese university will help them advance in the future. Some students in the Taiwanese university track reported, matter-of-factly, "Chinese should go to Chinese schools."

Although a homogeneous group, the Korean-Huaqiaos developed varying degrees of ethnic identity based on the extent to which their group identity is salient and significant to their college choice. The analysis of interviews revealed that Taiwanese university-track students seemed to have a clear sense of belonging to their Chinese heritage, while Korean university-track students feel confused and conflicted about their identity. Some Taiwanese university-track students expressed strong and positive emotional ties to their Chinese heritage, whereas some Korean university-track students desired to adapt to and be accepted by Korean society. Taiwanese university-track students were more interested in learning of their ethnic and cultural heritage than their Korean university-track counterparts, who feel that ethnicity is less important in their lives than cultural linguistic identity.

The Huaqiaos constantly negotiate their identity according to their perceived needs. These attitudes and behaviors have important implications for the ways in which the Korean-Huaqiaos live their lives, interact with Korean society, and view their opportunity, all of which influences their college choices. During the 1970s and early 1980s, the major trend was to identify more closely with their ethnic heritage, while from the late 1980s up to the present a more acculturated model is indicated.

The Effect of Gender on College Choice

One interesting contrast within this population group was that the majority of female students attended the Taiwanese university track while the majority of male students chose the Korean university track. This gender discrepancy in college choice reflects the Huaqiao community's belief about college's function, which for male students is to "prepare to take over their father's business," while for female students it is to "meet suitable marriage partners." While a male Huaqiaos' marriage to a Korean female is acceptable, based on the notion that a Korean female can be "emulated into Huaqiao culture," the Huaqiao community frowns upon a Huaqiao female's marriage to a Korean male because in such a case the Huaqiao female is expected to emulate Korean culture. For this reason, most female Huaqiao students chose the Taiwanese university-track and hoped to settle down in Taiwan. These attitudes are consistent with interviews with parents, who believe in general that their daughters will be happier by marrying Taiwanese men who are culturally Chinese and financially more affluent than Korean-Huaqiaos.

However, a growing number of female Huaqiao students are entering Korean universities, and thus there is increasing intermarriage between Huaqiao females and Korean males. According to an observer, this phenomenon is a result of a change in family structure — from an extended family system, with many children, to the nuclear family, with only a couple of children. Thus, with fewer children, parents are less willing to send them away. Many of the Korean university-track female students reported their parents' concern that they might marry a Korean. Still other students reported that although their parents prefer a Chinese man, a "good Korean" is acceptable. This change in attitude is in stark contrast to the reports from the 1970s, when the majority of marriageable female Korean-Huaqiaos migrated to Taiwan, causing demographic changes and thus altering the dynamics of the Korean-Huaqiao community.

For male students, the prospect of inheriting the family business was another significant reason for choosing Korean universities. These students recognized the importance of building a human connection with the broader society. Entrance to the prestigious universities [some students noted] would enhance the building of "alumni connections," a reflection of Korean society's "diploma disease," nepotism, and regionalism.

Among the male students, military service was another important consideration in choosing a Korean university. The Huaqiaos reported that male Huaqiaos must serve two years in the military when they graduate from a Taiwanese university if they wish to remain in Taiwan. Otherwise, they must return to Korea for two years in order to become eligible to request permission to reside in Taiwan. Parental concern about their sons marrying Korean females was not expressed in the remarks of Korean university-bound Huaqiao male students.

Social Needs for Korean Universities

Sorensen (1986) correctly notes that the educational system of present-day South Korea not only reflects a practical need to train an efficient work force, but also must respond to students' and parents' demands for upward mobility through education. Further, he notes Koreans' tendency to define status and self in relation to the group — family, lineage, and nation — to which they belong.

The majority of the Huaqiao students answered that going to college is "a practical necessity," not only for getting a job but also for the social recognition in status-conscious Korean society. Huaqiaos believe that without a college education, their standing in Korea will be further reduced. Therefore, even those who are academically less able students plan to take advantage of the stress-free admission examination for foreign students, and to receive some college education. Some students pointed out the relatively easier entrance examination requirement as a reason for choosing a Korean university. One student, who did not want to live in Taiwan, admitted that he planned to attend a Korean university while he figured out what he wanted to do. He remarked,

> I am glad that I could go to a prestigious Korean university without taking competitive exams with Korean students. I know I can't pass the Korean university exam if I am to take it with Korean students.

Many of the Huaqiao parents acknowledged the benefit of their children not suffering "examination hell" like their Korean counterparts and also declared that they cannot afford to pay the exorbitant cost that Korean parents are paying for their children's cram schools and/or tutoring. For this reason, some Huaqiao parents informed me that they are holding off on pursuing naturalization in spite of other benefits they would receive as Korean citizens.

Reflecting this peculiar academic environment in which Korean-Huaqiaos are situated, Huaqiao students are highly concentrated in areas such as foreign languages (Japanese and English are most popular) and Business, which can be translated into a mobile occupational opportunity. Academically able students are in medicine or Chinese medicine, and virtually no students study law, natural science, political science, or social science.

The Influence of Ethnic Education on College Choice

There were differing views between the Korean university-track students and Taiwanese university-track students with regard to the impact of ethnic education on their lives. Ethnic education appeared to have a greater influence on those who are in the Taiwanese university-track, for learning the Chinese language and culture instilled in them a sense of ethnic identity. On the other hand, Korean university-track students reported a greater influence from Korean popular culture and the mass media. These students conceded that Korean cultural influence is so vast that in spite of twelve years of ethnic education in Chinese they feel their command of the Chinese language and culture is inadequate. The following view was frequently repeated by other interviewees.

> Although I have been educated in Chinese schools for twelve years, I am not fluent in Chinese. The fact that I am Chinese but can't speak Chinese fluently makes me very embarrassed. So, I am not an authentic Chinese but not a Korean citizen either. I am a Korean-Huaqiao who falls between the two worlds.

Another student related,

> I have been educated at Chinese schools but I am more familiar with Korean language and culture. Still, everybody tells me I am Chinese, so I guess I am a Chinese person who lives in Korea.

Many others expressed a similar sentiment. Their inadequacy with the Chinese language and their lack of knowledge about Chinese culture made them uneasy about identifying themselves as Chinese.

Family environment seemed to play a significant role in the development of ethnic identity. Most Korean university-track students, even those with ethnic Chinese parents, reported the language of communication at home as Korean. During a group discussion, one of the interviewees was surprised to find out her best friend's mother was ethnic Chinese. She exclaimed, "I thought your mother was Korean. She always speaks Korean." This is not an isolated case, as it might have been twenty years ago, but rather is commonplace. Bombarded by the Korean culture and media, ethnic Chinese parents said, "We give up. We aren't even thinking about language purity. Communication in Chinese is difficult. There is no way we can translate everything the kids watch on TV into Chinese. It is much simpler to speak Korean." Such a situation has been progressively increasing, so that now over eighty percent of elementary first-graders speak no Chinese at all when they enter school. Recollecting their elementary school days, when most of the students were able to speak Chinese, teachers in elementary school said "We have to give instructions in Korean to teach Chinese to these children." Since the disappearance of Chinatowns during the '70s and '80s, due to the urban planning measures of the Korean government, it is today not only difficult to find community support for Chinese cultural activities, but most parents have to forego the convenience of neighborhood ethnic schools in the heart of Chinatown and endure long commutes. Still, for many parents, ethnic education is the only means of providing their children with a Chinese identity.

The fluid and complex nature of identity was revealed in this study. Some students tend to identify themselves along ethnic lines, while others give greater importance to their cultural identity. These seemingly contrasting ways of expressing who they are in essence based on the same principle: identification along linguistic lines, that is, the language the students feel more comfortable with. Those who are prefer Chinese tend to identify themselves more strongly as Chinese and to choose Taiwanese universities, contemplating relocation, while those who prefer Korean identify themselves more closely with Koreans, choose Korean universities, and plan to live in Korea.

Gender Effect

The decrease of the Huaqiao population had another effect: further investigation revealed that female Korean-Huaqiaos traditionally favored Taiwanese universities, and during the 1970s and 1980s the gender imbalance between the tracks became even more pronounced. The interview's revealed that a greater number of female Huaqiaos absolutely and proportionally went to Taiwan during the 1970s and 1980s, which caused a gender imbalance among Huaqiaos of marriageable age. According to an interviewee, "Most of my alumni friends in Taiwan are females . . . about eighty percent."

Increased intermarriage between the two ethnic groups, especially between Huaqiao males and Korean females, occurred as a natural outcome of the exodus of female Huaqiaos to Taiwan. According to an interviewee,

> There are lots of intermarriages between Huaqiaos [male] and Koreans [female] now because most Chinese females of marriageable age went to Taiwan. . . . At alumni gatherings I found about seventy percent of the male alumni are married to Korean women.

Such comments are commonly heard. Another interviewee confirmed this:

> In the past there were very few Chinese women who were married to Korean men. Now it has changed dramatically. Many Huaqiao women are marrying Koreans, and more than half of our male graduates are marrying Korean women.

It was explained that female Huaqiaos' migration to Taiwan was largely due to the lack of job opportunities and the concentration of Korean-Huaqiaos in the restaurant business, a factor that limited this minority's social mobility. According to Mr. Z,

> They [Huaqiao females] did not want to remain in Korea. All the female Huaqiaos went to Taiwan. They thought the most they could do here in Korea was the Chinese restaurant business and

they despised it. We were not studious, and in the exam we barely passed. The girls saw no future in that, so they left for Taiwan. The parents were eager to send their children away and the children were obsessed with getting away.

Disclosing that he is married to a Korean, he mischievously remarked, "You can't just fly to Taiwan and say, 'I am looking for a bride!'"

Although to lesser in degree than during the 1970s, my survey in 1998 at SOCHS showed a higher female concentration in the Taiwanese university-track (see table 3)

	Korea University Track		Taiwan University Track	
	Number	(%)	Number	(%)
Male (N=78)	62	(80)	14	(18)
Female (N=58)	23	(40)	35	(60)

Table 3: Choice of Korea and Taiwan Universities by Gender of SOCHS Seniors, 1999

Female students' concentration in the Taiwanese university track was absolutely and proportionally greater: eighty percent male and forty percent female students in the Korean university track, and eighteen percent male and sixty percent female students in the Taiwanese university track.

Taiwanese university-track females responded that stronger family support led to their decision to attend college in Taiwan. An interesting point of contention is that although a greater proportion of Korean university-track female students indicated future career options as their primary consideration for choosing a Korean institution, family influence may be greater among this population as an analysis of the interviews revealed that "wanting to be with family" as equally great among Korean university-bound female students. Korean university-track male students reported receiving more parental support in their college choices than their Taiwanese university-track male counterparts. A greater number of Korean university-track students who claim that their college choice was independent of family influence were evident for both Korean and Taiwan university tracks and both genders. Interviews with Korean university-track female students revealed that although they made their own decisions, their parents were concerned that they might become acquainted with Korean boys at the university and ultimately marry them. However, the degree of such concern seems slight compared to a generation ago. Thus, the preference for Taiwanese universities by Korean-Huaqiao females reflects their parents' concern about marriage prospects. On the contrary, male Huaqiaos' marriages to Korean females were more accepted. According to a parent,

> My daughters prefer to go to Taiwan for college, and I strongly support that idea. I prefer them to stay in Taiwan and marry Chinese. That is a practical reason. If they were boys, I would want them to stay here, and be educated in Korean universities and take over my business. To succeed in Korea, a Korean university is essential, but, for girls, I think it is better to go to Taiwan.

Another interviewee echoed her thoughts, saying,

> My daughter is in the Taiwanese university track. I insisted she go to Taiwan. I am not concerned too much with ethnic issues, but my husband is. It is a bit too early, but he is warning the children against interethnic marriage.

Although male students are entering Korean universities, the trend is still that female students go to Taiwan. This is seen as the best choice for a woman because a "female's status in Taiwan is better than in Korea." Another interviewee elaborates:

> My mother considered all these factors, and sent my sisters, both younger and older, to Taiwan for study, and they all married Taiwanese men and are living there. [My elder and younger brothers are living in the United States. I am quite happy about the arrangements.] I don't think any Chinese girl will regret that her parents sent her to Taiwan for study and to find a husband there.

Hauqiao parents were convinced that women's positions are better in Taiwan than in Korea, often claiming,

> Taiwanese men are gentle, most couples work together, and there is no obligation to in-laws as in Korea. Housekeeping is much simpler as women don't have to cook. Quite often they [Taiwanese] eat-out as it is more cost efficient.

An interviewee candidly disclosed that

> [Increasing numbers of Huaqiao females are marrying Korean males but] it seems that the Chinese community is ready to take a Korean daughter-in-law but not a Korean son-in-law yet. They think the Korean male is less family-oriented and less considerate of his spouse.

In interviews, Huaqiao females who are married to Korean males claimed that these stereotypes have no basis, and that modern Korean males are equally compatible and family-oriented. Further, a Korean male, in general, has an advantage of economic security — being married to a Korean is much more comfortable socially — one is not bound by the restrictions that foreigners endure. It seemed that one interviewee's candid remark about the issue represent the underlying Huaqiao psychology regarding marriage between Huaqiao females and Korean males as a strategy of ethnic survival.

> If a Huaqiao male marries a Korean female, then the offspring will be Chinese and we can educate them. If a Huaqiao female marries a Korean male, then [the opposite is true and] we will disappear.

Yet, Huaqiaos like to boast that

> I think the best way for a Chinese man is to go to a Korean university, to succeed in Korean society, and to marry a Chinese woman. If that is not possible and he falls in love with a Korean woman, then I think that the Korean lady is very, very lucky and will be happy. Most of all, Chinese men are more family-oriented, and further we [Huaqiaos] don't live with parents-in-law. . . . Generally speaking, in the Chinese community, we think if a Korean woman marries a Chinese man, then she is very lucky. On the other hand, if a Chinese woman is married to a Korean man, then often they are not that happy. Some are [happy], but most often they are not. We have a few ladies here in my office who are married to Korean men. Their marriages seem to be working out well. But for me, I will still send my daughter to Taiwan. No parents want their children to be unhappy. This is my personal opinion.

Considering the past chronic shortage of marriageable female Huaqiaos in Korea, however, it may be possible to surmise that these claims developed out of the need for ethnic preservation in an attempt to keep members within the ethnic community, rather than that they are based on fact.

According to an interviewee,

> I think the Huaqiao community is ready for Korean daughters-in-law but not Korean sons-in-law.

Along with the growing presence of Korean daughters-in-law, the community's increasing exposure to Korean popular culture threatens the continuity of Huaqiao culture among the younger generation Huaqiaos', whose attachment to China has eroded. Interviewees stated,

> The younger generation [Huaqiaos] became just like Koreans —
> culturally and ethnically, culturally because of the TV and growing
> up with Korean neighbor kids, ethnically because of massive inter-
> marriage . . .

The following interview unveiled additional insights:

> When I was attending school, having a Korean mother was not con-
> sidered modish. Maybe because of the lower educational [socio-eco-
> nomic] level of Korean mothers. Then, Korean mothers were eager
> to learn Chinese and speak better Chinese [than their present
> counterparts], and assimilated into Chinese way of life. . . . But now
> these young mothers are not learning Chinese. Before, in the large
> family system, the mother- and father-in-law would speak Chinese.
> So the young bride would naturally be absorbed into the Chinese
> language and customs, but in the nuclear family I think it is more
> difficult.

In sum, the change has been more in the altered living environment
than in the actual number of intermarriages. Popular culture, such as
TV and radio, has become a strong force in absorbing the Huaqiao
youth into Korean pop culture. Further, the disappearance of
Chinatowns during the 1970s accelerated this process of
"Koreanization" by weakening community support. An interviewee
exclaimed,

> I feel all is changing. We are under pressure [through popular cul-
> ture] to assimilate to Korean society. Before, there was not much
> problem living in Korea and only speaking Chinese. Now, it is
> increasingly difficult to live here without speaking Korean.

Many of my interviewees expressed that the omnipresence of Korean
culture makes it very difficult to maintain the Chinese language and
culture, even for Huaqiao couples. One interviewee relates,

> Since the disappearance of Chinatowns, there is very little ethnic
> contact. All the neighbors are Koreans. Also more Huaqiao children
> are taking private lessons from Korean teachers or attend *Hakwon*
> [cram school]. The other factor is that fathers' jobs take lots of time
> away from home. They usually come home very late and, naturally,
> they speak Korean at home [most of them are second- or third-gen-
> eration Huaqiaos, and daily contacts with Koreans enable them to
> be fluent in Korean]. Even Chinese mothers speak Korean at home.
> It is much easier for them. Children play with neighborhood

> Korean kids and watch TV, etc. . . . Even grandparents who are sec-
> ond- or third-generation Huaqiaos are fluent in Korean.

Grandparents, who were first-generation immigrants, are forced to speak Chinese with their grandchildren because the older generation lacks fluency in Korean. This results in the older generation maintaining its ethnic identity, the fluency in Korean of younger generation parents and grandparents, has further accelerated the *Koreanization* of the present generation. In addition family structures changed from extended to nuclear.

The younger generation's inadequacy in the Chinese language has educational implications. According to the Principal of SOCHS,

> The younger generation Huaqiaos became just like Koreans because of TV and by growing up with Korean kids. In the past there were very few Chinese women who married Korean men. Now it has changed dramatically. Many Huaqiao women are marrying Korean men, and the majority of our male graduates are marrying Korean women. It means our next generation will be just like Koreans. This change became an educational issue. We foresaw this ten years ago. Our students are handicapped. They are neither fluent in Chinese nor in Korean. This is very difficult to overcome. Any kind of learning requires language fluency. Our new generation is not fluent in Chinese. This language problem makes it very difficult to study.

The students' inadequate command of the Chinese language was reflected in the words of a parent who is also a teacher:

> My daughter's classroom teachers told me that she is an excellent student. But I know she is not. I am a teacher and also fluent in Chinese. When I help her with homework, again and again I notice that she doesn't have a grasp of Chinese and thus does not really understand the instructions.

Another teacher responded,

> In Korea, Huaqiao education is more or less a bilingual education. We often speak a mixed language of Korean and Chinese. We use lots of Korea phrases and/or vocabulary in our conversation.

This comment is inaccurate in a way because the curriculums of Huaqiao schools are strictly Taiwanese, with the exception of that of SOCHS, which in 1996 adapted the Korean curriculum for the Korean university-track students (eleventh and twelfth grade) only. This remark also conflicts with those of other teachers who claim that younger generation students are fluent in neither Korean nor Chinese. Further, this teacher's observation contradicts the claims of many students who claim fluency in one language over another. It appears that inconsistency between colloquial and academic language is due to two different socialization processes, one in the family and one at school.

Institutional Accommodations

For decades, Huaqiao schools concentrated on the Taiwanese curriculum. One graduate facetiously said he was treated like a stepchild because of his decision to apply to an unpopular Korean university during the '70s. Another interviewee concurred,

> Until recently, the Taiwanese curriculum was chosen for both the Korean university-track and the Taiwanese university-track. The curriculum of the Korean university track was the same as that of the Taiwanese university-track. The only difference was that there were six Korean language classes per week for the Korean university track, while there were two classes per week for the Taiwanese university track. There was no other class which would prepare us for Korean universities. Everyone was left to his or her own resources.

Even for the Korean university track, subjects such as Korean history, geography, and government were not taught, and the Korean language was treated as the student's second foreign language after English. As one interviewee put it,

> We weren't even prepared to have an intelligent conversation with Korean students. We [Huaqiao students] weren't even equipped with basic knowledge about Korea . . . no knowledge in Korean history and geography. Although we were born and grew up in Korea, our Korean was only good for the market place. I didn't even understand when my classmates at the college were joking, and could not participate in any serious conversations/discussions . . .

Korean-Huaqiaos claim that this gross academic neglect of the needs of Korean university-track students by Huaqiao high schools resulted in high attrition rates among those admitted to Korean institutions. Interviewees assert that concentrating on the Taiwanese curriculum while living in Korea led to the maladjustment within the broader society. Consequently, the Huaqiao community deteriorated because it failed to produce intellectuals who could be advocates for its own cause.

The Huaqiao population considers that the shift toward Korean universities by Huaqiao students began in 1992 — the year of the Korean government's diplomatic switch from Taiwan to China. However, document analysis from the Seoul Overseas Chinese High School, which compiled data from 1986 to the present, showed a more comprehensible picture of the recent trend. The data indicates that in 1987 a greater number of Korean-Huaqiao students elected the Korean university track (Seoul Overseas Chinese High School, 1998).

The generation gap was noted as an explanation for the reasons for "Taiwan Fever" until the late 1980s. The parents recounted hostile Korean policies, especially economic policies, as the major reason for sending their children to Taiwan at that time, while students themselves claimed that the Taiwanese education itself was the major reason they chose this schooling.

Korean universities gradually gained popularity in the early 1980s as Korea made economic progress and grew politically stable. The first swing in this direction occurred in 1987, marking a dramatic 24.2 percent increase in Huaqiao students enrollment in the Korean university-track from the previous year. Then it showed a temporary setback in 1988. Although there was an increase in the total number of Korean university-track students, from ninety-six from the previous year to 102, there was an 11.5 percent decrease in the proportion. Therefore, it is difficult to characterize the 1980s, as there was a definite increase in the demand for the Korean university-track, yet the change was rather volatile. Nineteen ninety-two (1992) marks the turning point, and the Korean university-track began to regain popularity, this time more gradually but steadily.

Chapter Eight
Findings and Conclusion

Introduction

This study documents an important shift in the college choice patterns of Korean-Huaqiaos. Operating as *de facto* schools in the absence of clear policies governing the education of foreign nationals, the Huaqiaos' education in Korea from the 1950s through the present focused on education, which was based on the Taiwanese educational model. Prepared with a strong sense of ethnic identity and fluency in the Chinese language, graduates of these ethnic Chinese high schools before the 1990s predominantly chose Taiwanese colleges. Admission to Taiwanese universities was often utilized as a way to emigrate to Taiwan and bring the remaining family members from Korea upon graduation. The ethnic Chinese in Korea claim that discriminatory Korean policies led to the emigration of the Korean-Huaqiaos. Further, the majority of the remaining Korean-Huaqiaos have been undecided about staying in Korea, while strongly defining themselves by their ethnic identity. Since the early 1990s, however, trends have changed, and now the majority of Huaqiao students are entering Korean universities. This altered trend in college choice has been accompanied by the stabilization of the Huaqiao population in Korea.

Background

Korea, with a very small number of minorities, is known as one of the most homogeneous societies in the world. As one of the Newly Industrialized Countries (NIC), Korea has experienced an influx of guest workers since the 1980s, yet relatively few became long-term residents. The ethnic Chinese who arrived in Korea at the turn of the twentieth century, therefore, represent the single largest ethnic minority group, yet they comprise less than one percent of the total population. According to the Korean Ministry of Justice's 1996 *Annual Report of Statistics on Legal Migration*, there are 23,282 ethnic Chinese residing in Korea as legal aliens. Moreover, many Korean-Huaqiaos estimate that about 7,000 to 8,000 Huaqiaos are floating members, residing elsewhere while keeping resident alien status in Korea. Thus, the actual number of ethnic Chinese in Korea is approximately 15,000 with some estimates as low as 10,000 (*The Economist*, 1996). A study by Poston, Jr., Mao, & Yu (1994) indicated that Korea had the greatest loss of its ethnic Chinese population - seven percent - during the 1980s. This pattern of population decrease, due to Chinese emigration rather than to the effects of low fertility or high mortality, was halted in the 1990s. The choice of a Taiwanese university education and subsequent emigration was the main cause of population loss in the 1970s and '80s. The shift in the '90s to the choice of Korean colleges has led to more stability in the ethnic Chines population in Korea. This study has sought to understand the forces behind this shift in college choice trends.

Theoretical Framework and Summary of Findings

The research in this study has drawn on two bodies of literature: that of majority-minority relations and that of college choice. Research into ethnicity primarily focuses on power relations between ethnic groups. College choice research is inclined, however, to focus on one's individualistic bias in decision making. Drawing from other studies (Alexander and Eckland 1975; Hearn 1991; Karen 1988; and Thomas 1979) McDonaugh (1997, p. 4) concludes that "for all students, academic achievement remains the most important determinant of whether and where they go to college," adding that "systematic relationships exist within achievement groupings between income and college selectivity." The influence of factors such as socioeconomic background translate into "cultural capital" and "habitus" (Bourdieu, 1977; McDonough et al., 1997; Hearn, 1984; 1991; DiMaggio, 1982), academic achievement (DiMaggio and Powell, 1983; Schurenberg, 1989), individual expectation and motivation (Hearn, 1984), and gender (Alexander and Eckland, 1997; Hearn, 1991). In her multivariate analyses, McDonough (1994, p. 5) suggests "a hierarchy of effects of background characteristics on educational attainment . . . from strongest to weakest, is social class, race, and gender." All research focused college choice on individual inclination primarily between universities within a national system.

Marshall notes that "Citizenship is a status bestowed on those who are full members of a community. All who possess the status are equal with respect to the rights and duties with which the status is endowed" (Marshall and Bottomore, 1992, p. 18). For Marshall "the rights of the citizen . . . is the right to equality of opportunity" (p. 64), and further, the "equality of status is more important than equality of income" (p. 56).

According to Marshall (1950; 1992) citizenship consists of three elements: "civil", "political," and "social." The civil element is "composed of the rights necessary for individual freedom - liberty of the person, freedom of speech, thought and faith, the right to own property and to conclude valid contracts, and the right to justice" (Marshall, 1950; Marshall and Bottomore, 1992, p. 8). Marshall maintains that the right to justice is "the right to defend and assert all one's rights on terms of equality with others and by due process of law" through the courts of justice. The political element of citizenship is "to participate in the exercise of political power, as a member of a body invested with political authority or as an elector of the members of such a body," such as parliament and councils of local government. On the other hand, the social element "range[s] from the right to a modicum of economic welfare and security to the right to share to the full in the social heritage and to live the life of a civilised being according to the standards prevailing in the society. The institutions most closely connected with it are the educational system and the social service" (Marshall and Bottomore, 1992, p. 8).

However, "There is no universal principle that determines what those rights and duties shall be, but societies in which citizenship is a developing institution create an image of an ideal citizenship against which achievement can be measured and towards which aspiration can be directed" (Marshall and Bottomore, 1992, p. 18). Noting that "Citizenship defines the relationship between individuals and the state," Klausen (1995, p. 249) drawing from other studies asserted that "the process of state building affects the norms of citizenship" (Brubaker, 1995; Hobsbawm, 1993 in Klausen, 1995, p. 249). For example, a person who was born in 1917 and lived "in certain areas of Eastern Europe may have changed citizenship four or five times without ever having moved" (Hobsbawm, 1993 in Klausen, 1995, p. 249). As such, national boundaries and citizenship are altering as political changes are taking place. National boundaries and citizenship are therefore, subject to political changes.

In this study I have found it extremely useful to join the two literatures, majority-minority group relations and college choice, to bring the individual and the community together, for I have found that in the case of Korean-Huaqiaos a sense of ethnic identity affects college choice. Ethnic identity itself is a fluid concept that is strongly influenced by broader political, social, and economic forces, nationally and globally. My findings reflect this complexity, while at the same time giving greater clarity to the college choice process.

The Influence of Citizenship

Like national boundaries and citizenship, the majority-minority relationship within national boundaries is subject to change according to the political changes of internal and external factors. Consequently, ethnicity is fluid, subject to alteration according to the political strength of the involved parties. In the Korean-Huaqiaos' case, the relationship and relative political strength between Korea and China have acutely skewed the status of the minority population and, further, the minority population's reaction to Korean society. The majority-minority relationship, therefore, exhibits a group dimension of the power relationship, and individual identity fluctuates within this power relationship. At the beginning of immigration, the ethnic Chinese in Korea mainly identified themselves as simply "Chinese." Later on, this identity changed to "Chinese with Taiwanese nationality," for those who look up to Taiwan as their motherland. Recently this identity shifted, and the ethnic Chinese are now identifying themselves as "Korean-Huaqiaos," emphasizing their uniqueness from the Chinese in China, from the Chinese in Taiwan, and also from Koreans, yet stressing their ties to Korea. However, a relatively small minority of Huaqiaos identify themselves as Korean with Chinese ancestry as opposed to Chinese living in Korea or just Chinese.

The Influence of Legal Status

Marshall's (1950; 1992) concept of three elements of citizenship rights - civil, political, and social - is useful in determining citizenship rights. However, his concept of citizenship rights is limited to citizens; the rights of non-citizens are still ambiguous and a point of controversy in most countries. Gallstone, (1993 in Klausen, 1995, p. 249) notes that "sense of the community" and "loyalty" are associated with "communitarian views of rights and obligation in the democratic state," thus suggesting the "belonging requires the consent of the community" (Kalusen, 1995, p. 250). Klausen (1995) contends that the modern "welfare state has in effect intensified the importance of belonging to these communities" as a result of the elevated level of the state's obligation toward its citizens. As Korea becomes an ever more industrialized nation, the issue of citizenship is expected to become increasingly complex.

As was established in the Korean nationality law section of this study, Huaqiaos are precluded from Korean nationality through a citizenship law which emphasizes an individual's "blood," specifically patrilineal blood. Such a nationality law is not pragmatic when considering that a person who no longer lives in Korea but who also was born in another country with a Korean father is entitled to Korean citizenship. At the same time, foreign residents, who have lived in Korea for generations, are still considered foreign nationals. Such impracticality is exemplified in those children of mixed union, when Korean nationality law keeps them in a state of limbo, especially the children of Korean mothers and Huaqiao fathers. While these children culturally, linguistically, and biologically identify themselves as Koreans, they are a foreign population. Legal preclusion from Korean citizenship appears to induce Korean-Huaqiaos to associate closer with their Chinese identity. These findings coincide with Gosling's (1983) findings in a study of the Chinese in Southeast Asian countries regarding how government policy affects Chinese identity. For Korean-Huaqiaos, exclusion from citizenship magnifies their ethnic identity, which shapes college choices.

The Influence of Geopolitical Change

Vermenlen and Pels (1984) state that one dimension of ethnicity is "historical." The historical dimension, they assert "offers interpretations of the past." At the same time, it provides "an 'answer' to a specific situation [which] can be only understood as being influenced by historical experience" (p. 281). The study challenges Ogbu's definition of "voluntary minority" and "involuntary minority" by suggesting that "voluntary minority" and "involuntary minority" status are flexible relative to political change. The study, however, is closely aligned with the view of Nagel (1994, p. 152) who asserts that "the construction of ethnic identity and culture is the result of both structure and agency - a dialectic played out by ethnic groups and the larger society."

A change in Korean-Huaqiaos' status in Korea, therefore, is an indication of geopolitical changes occurring in the Korean peninsula rather than tangible changes in legal standing, leaving much to the interpretation and/or implementation of existing policies. As stated earlier, the Chinese people's immigration to Korea began in the nineteenth century, when China's role in Korea was rapidly waning. At the same time, newly industrialized Japan's control over Korea was steadily increasing. Anti-Japanese feelings among Koreans manifested in the Immo Military Revolt in 1882. The Korean King, Kojong, sought the presence of the Chinese military to counterbalance the rising Japanese influence in Korean peninsula. The Qing government obliged by sending Chinese soldiers as well as Chinese merchants to procure military supplies for their soldiers. Japanese objection soon led to the withdrawal of the Chinese soldiers in Korea, but some of the Chinese merchants returned and began to conduct trade. These merchants represented the first group of Chinese immigrants to Korea.

Due to Korea's earlier political subordination to China, these merchants had an advantage over Korea. Ethnic Chinese during this time maintained a semi-colonial status over Koreans, reflecting the lesser political status of Korea in relationship to China. Subsequent colonization of Korea by Japan from 1910 to 1945 manifested itself in the Chinese detachment from Korean society. In addition, the geographical proximity between Korea and China encouraged the frame of mind that the Chinese were sojourners, who would return to China when they saved enough money. Korean independence in 1945 brought drastic changes in the status of the two groups: Koreans were sovereigns of an independent nation and Huaqiaos were foreign nationals. Korean policies of the newly independent Korea focused on the interests of Korean citizens. China's involvement in the Korean War as an aid to the North, and Taiwan's support for the South Korea complicated the Huaqiaos' status in Korea. The Korean government pursued a staunch anti-communism policy, which was thus anti-China. Korea's political alliance with Taiwan, which claimed to be the legitimate successor to the "Republic of China,"forced Korean-Huaqiaos to accept Taiwan as the representative government of China, and, thus, their motherland until it would someday recover the mainland. Korean-Huaqiaos acquired Taiwanese nationality, based on the patrilineal nationality laws practiced by both Korea and both Chinas, which left them foreigners.

During this time, the Korean government heavily restricted the economic activities of foreign nationals, like the Korean-Huaqiaos, while leaving education to the Huaqiao community's own arrangement. Influenced by these political developments, Huaqiaos replicated the Taiwanese school system to educate their younger generations. This Taiwanese educational system politically oriented Huaqiaos toward Taiwan, enabled the Huaqiao youth to study in Taiwanese universities, and served as a grafting mechanism into Taiwan society for Korean-Huaqiaos. The Taiwan government, appreciative of the Overseas Chinese's economic strength, was ever attentive of Huaqiaos' educational desires and supported them through preferential admission, scholarships, and job placement upon graduation. Korean-Huaqiaos who were prepared by ethnic schools in the Chinese language, readily took advantage of the opportunity. Their beneficial affiliation with Taiwan is reflected, therefore, in their college choice.

Opportunity for some, however, worked to the detriment of others, for not all Huaqiaos were able to take advantage of this opportunity. For those who remained in Korea, their ethnic education appears to have brought further detachment from Korean society, leaving them further marginalized from the larger society. While academically able Huaqiao youth entered Taiwanese universities, those Huaqiao youth who remained in Korea were often ill prepared for the occupational world and Korean society. While limitation in social mobility caused the exodus of Korean-Huaqiaos to Taiwanese universities, it demoralized the remaining Huaqiaos, who felt helpless about their futures and mistrustful of the Korean government. Although it began as protection of Koreans coming out of colonial rule, restrictions on economic activities of Huaqiaos may have done a disservice to the Korean government, as Huaqiaos claimed that wealthy Huaqiaos emigrated to Taiwan or the United States resulting in a loss of human resources and capital.

This continued until the early 1990s, when Huaqiaos began to believe that in a booming Korean economy Huaqiao youth who studied at Korean universities faired better than those who studied and remained in Taiwan. Further, in 1992, a diplomatic switch-over occurred from Taiwan to China by the Korean government. As a newly industrialized nation seeking its own place in the community of nations, the diplomatic switch-over from Taiwan to China was viewed in Korea as having a dual benefit: gaining political advantage by neutralizing China from allegiance with the North Korea of the past, and gaining economic benefit by opening the massive Chinese market to Korea's booming industries. While most Huaqiaos remained as Taiwanese citizens, Shim (1992) notes that the diplomatic switch-over by the Korean government created an "identity crisis" among Korean-Huaqiaos, and the Huaqiao community became divided into "pro-China" and "pro-Taiwan" alignment. This division is visible; the younger generation Huaqiaos, who were educated in the Taiwanese style, tend to be politically and culturally aligned closely to Taiwan, while the older generation who have memories of "home" are more likely to be dedicated to China.

At the same time, "separatists" came into greater power in Taiwan, hoping to become independent of China. Taiwan, thus, became more responsive to Taiwanese needs, with less emphasis given to the wishes of the Overseas Chinese. Such a development in Taiwan discouraged the Overseas Chinese from settling in Taiwan. Korean-Huaqiaos believe the Korean government has been more sensitive toward Huaqiaos since the diplomatic renewal with China, and this softening of posture toward the Huaqiaos by the Korean government is propelled by China's political strength. Since distancing from Taiwan and having more options open to them, Huaqiaos more closely identify themselves with Korea, which in turn has had an effect on their college choices.

The Influence of an Ethnic Education

Through their own separate education system, which was sheltered from Korean influence, the Korean-Huaqiaos maintained a high degree of group cohesion through transmission of ethnic language and culture. Ethnic education, thus, safeguarded the ethnic identity of the Korean-Huaqiaos and has had a profound impact on college choice. This finding corresponds with Guskin's (1968) assertion that education plays an important role in either assimilating emigrants into the host country or maintaining ethnic identity. Further, Gosling notes that the policies of a given country influence the degree of acculturation and assimilation of its ethnic minorities. For example, open access to Thai education for the ethnic Chinese in Thailand, combined with restriction on Chinese education, expedited the high degree of assimilation/acculturation of the Thai-Chinese in Thailand. However, the Malaysian-Huaqiao policy combination of allowing limited access to ethnic education while favoring Malaysians in the economic arena resulted in the slowing of Huaqiaos integration into the larger society.

Although Huaqiao schools in Korea are operated in a *de facto* manner, current Korean educational policies benefit those who study in ethnic schools by allowing them to enter Korean universities as *"extra-quorum"* students, i.e., without having to take a competitive examination which Korean students must take. On the other hand, those Huaqiao youth who study in Korean schools must take the competitive examination like the Korean students. This Korean policy has encouraged the Huaqiaos to focus on ethnic education rather than assimilate into Korean society.

Ironically, the policy regarding Huaqiao education and college admission for those who graduate from Huaqiao schools is detrimental to Huaqiao education. Interviews with Huaqiao youth reveal that there is an incomplete linguistic transition from Korean to Chinese, even after twelve years of ethnic education in Chinese. Many Huaqiao youth admit that their Chinese is not adequate while their Korean is limited to a colloquial level, which is inadequate for college education or employment. Huaqiaos claim that Korean culture, especially the influence of TV combined with economic forces, are so strong that complete acquisition and transition to Chinese is practically impossible. Thus, the Huaqiao community must consider alternative educational options which will benefit the Huaqiao youth's adjustment in the larger society.

The Influence of Market Pressures and Rewards

It is well established that further financial reward is one of the most powerful motivations for college choice. In *The Chinese in Southeast Asia*, Gosling (1983, p. 1) observes that "ethnic identity would be weakened as national capitalist economic development (as opposed to colonial capitalist economic development) proceeded, and that class identity and divisions would replace ethnic identity and divisions." In a similar manner, Sow's (1983) study of Chinese in Malaysia reports that an increasing number of Chinese are converted to Islam in the desire to gain "membership in the national culture," which will also bring material reward. In discussing what Hechter (1984) terms as a "cultural division of labor," Vermeulen and Pels assert that "concentration of an ethnic group in specific class or socio-economic stratum or in a particular occupation or cluster of occupations may provide a basis for intra-ethnic interaction and common interests and may influence the opinions and attitudes of outsiders towards the group's self-image" (p. 279).

The Korean-Huaqiaos' perceived economic opportunities played a significant role in the shift in college choice. Korean business, faced with "the practical necessity of intercultural communication" (*Journal of Business & Technical Communication*, October 1999) in dealing with the Chinese market, sought graduates of Huaqiao schools for postings in China and other Southeast Asian countries. The demand for a bilingual/bicultural (Korean and Chinese) labor force needed by the Chinese market brought about a shift in college choice by Korean-Huaqiaos from Taiwanese universities to Korean universities. This trend was lead by Samsung, Korea's biggest electronics conglomerate, which offered sixty million won (approximately US 70,000 dollars) in scholarships to Seoul Overseas Chinese High School. The thirty students a year who received the scholarships almost automatically found jobs with Samsung (Shim, 1999). Along with this, there has been a fast shift toward Korean universities by Huaqiao students and also curriculum changes in the SOCHS. Since 1996 juniors and seniors in the Korean university-track of the SOCHS receive instruction in Korean in all academic subjects.

In the past, Huaqiao community members claimed that the lack of social mobility and opportunity available to Huaqiaos in Korean society led them to choose Taiwanese universities. The data from SOCMS and SOCHS supports this claim; most Huaqiaos have low status jobs. More than half of the Korea-Huaqiaos are engaged in the Chinese restaurant occupation and about ten percent are in retail business. Approximately four percent are in Chinese medicine and tourism and hospitality. The remainder of the population is engaged in various sales and service industries, while one percent is in agriculture. This low percentage of agricultural workers is due to the Korean government's restriction on land ownership by foreign nationals. Other modern professions in which the Korean-Huaqiaos participate are: two percent each in teaching and employment by the Taiwanese government (mostly related to KMT), one percent in pharmacy, and 0.5 percent in Western medicine. Most of the employment opportunities are limited within the ethnic community. The Huaqiao community believes that the concentration in the restaurant business is even more intense in rural areas in Korea. Ju Boling, a Huaqiao writer, argues that Korean policies "condemn Huaqiaos to *Zzhazhangmyun jangsa*" (interview, 1999).

Zzhazhangmyun jangsa, literally meaning "selling of Chinese noodles," derogatorily refers to the Chinese restaurant business and Huaqiaos, since the majority of ethnic Chinese in Korea engage in this business. Many of the laws restricting Huaqiaos' economic activities have recently been abrogated and the shift of college choices by Korean-Huaqiao youth corresponds with this broadened opportunity. Therefore, this study concurs with other academic findings that perceived future economic gains play a greater role than affecting only college choice. In other words, this study finds that economic opportunities appear to be the greatest motivation for Korean-Huaqiaos' relocation or willingness to assimilate.

The Influence of Generational Change

Many studies (Chan, 1987; Rogler, Cooney, & Ortiz, 1980) document "the shift in commitment to one's ethnic group over time, with a weaker ethnic identity among those who have lived longer in the new country" (Rosenthal and Feldman, 1992). Drawing from other studies (Connor 1977; Constaninou and Harvey, 1985; Fathi, 1972; Masuda, Hasegawa, & Matsumato, 1973; Masuda, Matsumato, and Meredith, 1970), Rosenthal and Feldman (1992) conclude, "generational differences in ethnic identity tend to show an erosion of ethnic identity in later generations of immigrants" (p. 215). Rosenthal and Feldman (1992) outline in other studies (Wooden, Leon, & Tashima, 1988) that "ethnic identity remains stable after the second generation" and "a resurgence occurs, with stronger identification occurring in third and subsequent generations" (Scourby, 1980; Ting-Toomey, 1981). Second generation Huaqiaos who have a strong sense of ethnic identity from their first generation immigrant parents, identified themselves fervently along ethnic lines; they preferred Taiwanese education. Current third and forth generation Huaqiaos, whose absorption into Korean language and culture is more complete, appear to have a diminished ethnic identity which leads to the shift in college choice among the younger generation Huaqiaos. The Korean-Huaqiaos' case of erosion of ethnic identity occurs among the third generation, suggesting that diminished ethnic identity is shaped by the changing context.

The intensity of cultural and linguistic identity with Korea is especially pronounced among the Huaqiaos who are biologically Korean through the maternal line. Such a development concerns older generation Huaqiaos regarding the survival of the ethnic language, value system, and community itself. Further, such a concern has been amplified recently since approximately half of the first graders in Seoul Overseas Chinese Elementary School and Chinese elementary schools in other locations are reported to have Korean mothers. This shift in the ethnic configuration within the Huaqiao community influences the college choice of Huaqiao youth toward Korean universities. Younger Huaqiaos' assertion of being identified as "Korean-Huaqiao" as opposed to the previous generation's ethnic "Chinese" or "Chinese with Taiwanese nationality" convey their growing bond to Korea. Additionally, it appears that with increased individualism and access to greater material affluence a greater number of younger generation Huaqiaos are making decisions on their own, including college choice, with less consideration for community pressure.

The Influence of Gender and Marriage Prospects

Changes in college choice appear, however, to be limited to male students; female Huaqiao students still tend to opt for Taiwanese universities. In regard to female Huaqiaos' college choice, the community influence is still in command. Female Huaqiaos are expected to go to a Taiwanese university and find a suitable marriage prospect. Such a practice has brought gross gender imbalance to the Huaqiao community. The Huaqiao community's attitude is that Huaqiao females should marry ethnic Chinese only, while Huaqiao males can marry Korean females and integrate their wives and offspring into Chinese culture. As a result, there is a gender gap among Huaqiaos in Korea. Because Huaqiao females elect to go to Taiwanese universities, intermarriage between Huaqiao males and Korean females has became greater than before, which presents educational dilemmas to the Huaqiao community. The findings of this study concur with Raybeck (1983) in his study of the Chinese community in Malaysia. He argues that the size of the

Chinese community, their economic role, local political policies, possibilities of intermarriage or availability of Chinese marriage partners, communication within the Chinese community, and the Chinese's perception of the local population all play a powerful role in whether or not they assimilate into the larger society. For Korean-Huaqiaos, who are few in numbers, economically weak, precluded from political participation, and have limited Chinese marriage partners (especially for males), the incentive to accommodate and even to assimilate becomes greater. Related to this is the earlier discussion that female Huaqiaos are encouraged to choose Taiwanese universities by parents seeking suitable marriage partners in Taiwan for their daughters. Huaqiao males and females are less attracted to each other than in earlier periods. Male Huaqiaos, who lack good prospects for social and occupational mobility, are not thought to be good mates. By the same token, male Huaqiaos' preference for a Korean female marriage partner hinges on economic benefit. In other words, a Korean wife can manage their property and conduct business. However, this kind of arrangement threatens ethnic continuation as younger Korean females who marry Huaqiaos uphold their Korean cultural identity, unlike their predecessors who assimilated into Chinese culture.

As stated earlier, the Huaqiao community's pressure on its youth seems to play an important factor in Huaqiao youths' college choice. In the past, the Huaqiao community served to reinforce its cultural and linguistic heritage. Yet, changes are occurring, as reflected in the opening of two tracks in the SOCHS in 1996, which indicated the Huaqiao community's desire to adapt to the larger Korean society. The authority of the ethnic community remains particularly powerful on female Huaqiaos.

In sum, the above mentioned factors are intimately intertwined in the formation of the current Huaqiaos' ethnic identity. Although the ethnicity of younger Korean-Huaqiaos appears diminished relative to the previous generations, it remains the most powerful shaper of identity for the Huaqiaos, and therefore, it is also the primary factor which drives all major life choices, including choices regarding higher education. The Chinese education in Korea was more about providing the Huaqiao population with the opportunity to learn and appreciate its Chinese heritage. Such education ill served Huaqiaos in adapting to mainstream Korean society. As one interviewee notes, maintenance of ethnic identity for Korean-Huaqiaos may be a "Pyrrhic victory." The Huaqiaos' focus on an ethnic education may lie in the fact that they had limited social mobility within Korean society as seen in their preclusion from citizenship and economic mobility. Perhaps, ethnic education was the only way left to express themselves, signifying Korea's failure to embrace them as part of the "national culture."

Limitation

This study has attempted to examine the Korean-Huaqiao community in the continuously changing world. Recognizing the lack of prior research, the qualitative research method was utilized to gather Korean-Huaqiaos' perspectives and their rationales for educational choices in the context of their social milieu. The issue of educational choice was used to examine the political, social, and cultural changes of the Korean-Huaqiaos. The main research site, SOCHS and the Seoul Huaqiao community, whom I was able to access through personal connections, may not represent the entire Huaqiao population in Korea. This study, which is specific to Korean-Huaqiaos, may also not be generalized to other settings. In addition, there has been difficulty in translating interviews, which were mostly conducted in Korean, into English. The difficulty arises mainly in the area of specific terms unique to the Korean or Huaqiao setting, for which there are not equivalent English terms. Further, nuances resulting from different interpretations of the languages complicated the translation process. Also, this study is limited to 1998. It may be too early to gauge the effects of post-1999 Korean policies in regard to Huaqiao population, which has become much more inclusive.

Implications for Further Study

The findings of this study have important implications; one implication is that under certain conditions, minority groups may opt to create important intervening devices, such as the establishment of specific schools that foster group identity, so much so that it has a powerful influence on individual choice. Also, there may be geopolitical constraints shaped by majority-minority relations that impact college choice, such as the conditions surrounding citizenship, ethnicity, and opportunity for geographical and socioeconomic mobility. To the extent that there are changes in these theoretically highlighted parameters, there appears to be shift in the group direction of college choice.

This study provides direction for future research. The impact of relaxed restriction on economic activities by Huaqiaos, including acquisition of real estate and pending changes in the nationality law, will have a profound impact on Korean-Huaqiaos' aspirations in Korea and their relationship to Korea. These changes point to an area for future research. The Huaqiao community's future response to the increasingly globalizing world and their definition of the role of ethnic education in such a context is also worthy of future research. Included should be the issue of high attrition by Huaqiao students in Korean universities; how Huaqiaos who graduated from Korean universities succeeded would be another useful research direction. Their coping mechanisms in Korean universities and their achievement in terms of socio-economic mobility are points of interest. This study will also provide tools to examine the ethnic Chinese in other settings. Studies of small minorities who are on the brink of losing economic, political, and socio-cultural autonomy in a larger homogeneous setting may benefit from this study. Finally, the cross-cultural studies mentioned above could be aligned with research conducted in North America to gain a deeper understanding of majority-minority relations, so as to create more responsive interethnic relations in an ever increasingly multiethnic, global society.

Conclusion

As with other extremely homogeneous and monocultural societies, Korean history is primarily linked to Korean national identity. Therefore, Korean identity has always been tied to the legal and political status of Korean citizens, which restricts others from "becoming" Korean (DeVos and Wagatsuma, 1995). Accordingly, the status of the Chinese ethnic minority living in Korea for generations is that of the foreigner. *Jus Sanguinis*, the recognition of nationality by birth, led the Korean government to acknowledge Korean-Huaqiaos only as foreign nationals. Unlike American society, which has a problem defining American identity due to its people's diverse origins, in Korean society, determination of who is a Korean citizen starts from the premise that Koreans are of a totally homogeneous origin (De Vos and Wagatsuma, 1995). Korean identity, based on the principle of lineage, appears to be impractical in the increasingly globalizing world. Exclusion from Korean society resulted in the Huaqiaos' preoccupation with ethnic education of the younger generation. In the past, there has been a restriction on the Huaqiaos' opportunities in Korean society, some being the result of this ethnic population's own international mechanisms.

Recently, a shift in college choice has taken place among Korean Huaqiaos to Korean universities from previously popular Taiwanese universities. These changes are an essentially adaptive reaction to both Taiwan and Korea's political, social, and economic reality. For instance, in Korea, the legislation for inclusion in citizenship for those whose mothers are Korean has been proposed and is pending approval from Korea's National Assembly. Furthermore, many restrictions on economic activities have been abrogated.

Economic growth in Korea has provided greater opportunities for all, including the Huaqiaos. Political openness, the reduced fear of war in the Korean peninsula, and the establishment of a diplomatic relationship with China have brought feelings of security to those whose roots originated in China. As trade with China began, the Korean-

Huaqiaos' knowledge of the Chinese language and culture, along with their Chinese connection, became invaluable to Korean companies seeking business in China.

An examination of the Huaqiao schools in Korea reflects many issues: ethnic attitudes, the interaction of the two societies, and, most of all, the Huaqiaos' perceptions of their opportunities. Beginning in 1996, the SOCHS made a number of changes to improve the opportunities for its graduates to assimilate into Korean society. Among the changes was the establishment of a Korean University-track at the junior level for those who plan to study at a Korean university or those who seek employment in Korea. For this endeavor the SOCHS hired Korean university-trained teachers, and increased the classes with Korean language instruction. The innovations, which were financed by Korean industries, induced greater demand for Korean universities among Korean-Huaqiaos.

The changes in a given organization's interests reflect external changes. In the case of the SOCHS, although limited to the Korean university-track, the new principal's vision changed SOCHS's general orientation - toward Korea. The principal, himself a second-generation Huaqiao educated in Huaqiao schools in Korea and a Taiwanese university, felt strongly that the Chinese living in Korea must define a new identity for themselves if they want to survive in Korea.

Yet, while the shift is taking place, some issues remains, such as whether ethnic education, which is apart from Korean reality and lacking in competitiveness when compared with Korean schools, are best for the Huaqiaos' adaptation in Korea. The Korean government needs to examine whether or not it is in the best interest of the Korean government to keep this population at a distance, though armed with a potent ethnic identity, instead of incorporating them into the "national culture."

References

Aitken, N. (1982). College Student Performance, Satisfaction and Retention: Specification and Estimation of a Structural Model. *Journal of Higher Education, 53*. 32-50.

Alexander, K. and Cook, M. (1979). The Motivational Relevance of Educational Plans: Questioning the Conventional Wisdom. *Social Psychology Quarterly*, 43. 202-213.

Alexander, K. and Eckland, B. (1975). Basic Attainment Processes: A Replication and Extension. *Sociology of Education*, 54, 457-495.

Alexander, K. and Eckland, B. (1977). High School Context and College Selectivity: Institutional Constraints in Educational Stratification. *Sociology Forces, 56*. 166-188.

Anderson, E. (1983). A View from the Bottom: The Rise and Decline of a Malaysian Chinese Town. In Gosling, P. and Lim, L. (Ed.), *The Chinese in Southeast Asia, 2*. 147-169. Singapore: Maruzen Asia.

Anyon, J. (1981). Social Class and School Knowledge. *Curriculum Inquiry*, 11. 3-42.

Anyon, J. (1980). Social Class and the Hidden Curriculum of Work. *Journal of Education*, 162. 67-92.

Anyon, J. (1981). Social Class and School Knowledge. *Curriculum Inquiry, 11* (1). 3-42.

Astin, A. (1993). *What Matters in College: Four Critical Years Revisited*. San Francisco: Jossey Bass.

Ballard, A. (1973). *The Education of Black Folk*. New York: Harper Colophon Books.

Barton, C. (1983). Trust and Credit: Some Observations Regarding Business Strategies of Overseas Chinese Traders in South

Vietnam. In Lim, L. and Gosling, P. (Ed.), *The Chinese in Southeast Asia, 1.* 46-64. Singapore: Maruzen Asia.

Bauer, T. and Zimmermann, K. (1997, Spring). Network Migration of Ethnic Germans. *International Migration Review, 31* (1). 143-149.

Bernstein, B. (1977). Social Class, Language, and Socialisation. In Karabel, J. andHalsey, A. (Ed.), *Power and Ideology in Education.* New York: Oxford University Press.

Best, J. and Kahn, J. (1986). *Research in Education* (5th ed.). Englewood Cliffs, NJ:Prentice-Hall.

Block, J. (1991). *Understanding Historical Research: A Search for Truth.* Glen Rock, NJ: Research Publications.

Bogdan, R., and Bilken, S. (1992). *Qualitative Research for Education: An Introduction to Theory and Methods* (2nd ed.). Boston: Allyn and Bacon.

Bond, M. and Yang, K. (1982). Ethnic Affirmation Versus Cross-Cultural Accommodation: The Variable Impact of Questionnaire Language on Chinese Bilinguals in Hong Kong. *Journal of Cross-Cultural Psychology,* 13. 169-185.

Borg, W., Gall, J., and Gall, M. (1993). *Applying Educational Research: A Practical Guide* (3rd ed.). New York: Longman.

Bosley, D. (1992, Winter). Broadening the Base of a Technical Communication Program: An Industrial/Academic Alliance. *Technical Communication Quarterly, 1,* 41-56.

Bourdieu, P. (1977). Cultural Reproduction and Social Reproduction, 487-511. In Karabel, J. and Halsey, A. (Ed.), *Power and Ideology in Education.* New York: Oxford University Press.

Bourdieu, P. and Passeron, J. (1977). *Reproduction in Education, Society, Culture.* Beverly Hills, CA: Sage.

Boyle, R. (1966). The Effect of High School on Student Aspirations. *American Journal of Sociology,* 71. 628-39.

Brint, S. and Karabel, J. (1989). *The Diverted Dream: Community Colleges and the Promise of Educational Opportunity in America, 1900-1985.* New York: Oxford University Press.

Brubaker, R. (1992). *Citizenship and Nationhood in France and Germany.* Cambridge: Cambridge University Press.

Brumberg, S. (1986). *Going to America, Going to School: The Jewish Immigrant Public School Encounter in Turn-of-the-Century New York City.* New York: Praeger.

Calson, R. (1987). *The Americanization Syndrome: A Quest for Conformity.* New York: St. Martin's Press.

Cardwell, J., and Hill, A. (1988). Recent Developments Using Micro-Approaches to Demographic Research. In J.C. Cardwell, Hill, A.G. and Hull, V. J. (Eds.), *Micro-Approaches to Demographic Research.* 1-9. Great Britain: Kegan Paul International.

Carstens, S. (1983). Pulai Hakka Chinese Malaysian: A Labyrinth of Cultural Identities. In Gosling, P. and Lim, L. (Ed.), *The Chinese in Southeast Asia, 2.* 99-125. Singapore: Maruzen Asia.

Chan, H. (1987). *The Adaptation, Life Satisfaction and Academic Achievement of Chinese Senior School Students in Melbourne.* Unpublished Doctoral Dissertation, Monash University: Melbourne, Australia.

Chan, P. (1983). The Political Economy of Urban Chinese Squatters in Metropolitan Kuala Lumpur. In Lim, L. and Gosling, P. (Ed.), *The Chinese in Southeast Asia, 1.* 232-244. Singapore: Maruzen Asia.

Chanda, N. (1992, September 3). Opening Moves. *Far Eastern Economic Review, 155* (35).

Changing Partners. (1992, August 29). *The Economist, 324* (7774).

Cheong S. (1992, Spring). A Study of the Origin of the Legal Status of Korean Residents in Japan: 1945-1951. *Korean Journal, 32* (1).

China's Diaspora Turns Homeward: Overseas Chinese Investment in China. (1993, November 27). *The Economist, 329* (7839).

Choi, H. (1994, Spring). Overseas Koreans and Their Adaptation Patterns. *Korea Journal, 34.*

Christian, J., et al. (1976). The Multidimensional and Dynamic Nature of Ethnic Identity. *International Journal of Psychology, 11.* 281-291.

Chun, A. (1989, April). Pariah Capitalism and the Overseas Chinese of Southeast Asia: Problems in the Definition of the Problem. *Ethnic and Racial Studies, 12* (2), 233-256.

CIA - The Word Factbook 1999. Retrieved December 1999, from the World Wide Web: *http://www.odci.gov/cia/publications/factbook*, 1999.

Clammer, J. (1983). Chinese Ethnicity and Political Culture in Singapore. In Gosling, P. and Lim, L. (Ed.), *The Chinese in Southeast Asia, 2.* 266-284. Singapore: Maruzen Asia.

Clark, M. (1965). *Overseas Chinese Education in Indonesia: Minority Group Schooling in an Asian Context.* Washington DC: U.S. Government Printing Office.

Cohen, D. (1970). Immigrants and the Schools. *Review of Educational Research, 40* (1). 13-27.

Cohen, J. and Arato, A. (1992). *Civil Society and Political Theory.* Cambridge, MA: MIT Press.

Cohen, L. and Manion, L. (1985). *Research Methods in Education* (2nd ed.). Dover, NE:Croom Helm.

Cohen, M. (1982). Changing Education Strategies Among Immigrant Generations: New York Italians in Comparative Perspective. *Journal of Social History, 15* (3). 443-466.

Cohen, R. and Mohl, R. (1979). *The Paradox of Progressive Education: The Gary Plan and Urban Schooling*. Port Washington, New York: Kennileat.

Connell, R., Ashenden, D. Kessler, S. and Dowsett, D. (1982). *Making the Difference: Schools, Families, and Social Division*. Sydney, Australia: G. Allen and Unwin.

Connor, J. (1977). *Tradition and Change in Three Generation of Japanese-Americans*. Chicago: Nelson-Hall.

Constantinou, S. and Harvey, M. (1985). Dimensional Structure and Intergenerational Differences in Ethnicity: The Greek Americans. *Sociology and Social Research, 69*. 234-254.

Cookson, P. and Persell, C. (1985). *Preparing for Power: America's Elite Boarding Schools*. NY: Basic.

Cowan, N. and Cowan, R. (1989). *Our Parents' Lives: The Americanization of Eastern European Jews*. New York: Basic Books.

Cummings, W. (1991). *Foreign Students, International Higher Education: An Encyclopedia, 1*. New York: London: Garland Publishing, Inc.

Daniels. J. (1920). *American Via the Neighborhood*. New York: Harper & Brothers.

Dash Moore, D. (1981). *At Home in America: Second Generation New York Jews*. New York: Columbia University Press.

Davidson, A. (1996). *Making and Molding Identity in Schools*. Albany: State University of New York Press.

Davidson, A., Yu, H. and Phelan, P. (1993). "The Ebb and Flow of Ethnicity:Constructing Identity in Varied School Settings. *Educational Foundations, 7* (l).65-87.

Delgado-Gaitan, C. & H. Trueba (1991). *Crossing Cultural Borders: Education for Immigrant Families in America*. London: Falmer Press.

Demo, D. (1990). Socialization and Racial Identity Among Black Americans. *Social Psychology Quarterly, 53* (4). 364-374.

DeVos, G. (1980). Ethnic Adaptation and Minority Status. *Journal of Cross-Cultural Psychology, 11*. 101-124.

DeVos, G. and Wagatsuma, H. (1995). Cultural Identity and Minority Status in Japan. In Romannucci-Ross, L. and DeVos, G. (Eds.). *Ethnic Identity*. Walnut Creek, CA: Altamira Press.

Deyo, F. (1983). Chinese Management Practices and Work Commitment in Comparative Perspective. In Gosling, P. & L. Lim (Ed.), *The Chinese in Southeast Asia, 2*. 215-230. Singapore: Maruzen Asia.

DiMaggio, P. (1982). Cultural Capital and School Success: The Impact of Status Culture Participation on the Grades of U. S. High School Students. *American Sociological Review, 47.* 189-201.

DiMaggio, P. and Powell, W. (1983). The Iron Cage Revisited: Isomorphism and Collective Rationality in Organizational Fields. *American Sociological Review, 48.* 147-60.

Doeringer, P. and Piore, M. (1971). *Internal Labor Markets and Manpower Analysis.* Lexington, MA: Heath.

Driedger, L. (1975). In Search of Cultural Identity Factors: A Comparison of Ethnic Students. *Canadian Review of Sociology and Anthropology, 12.* 150-162.

Driedger, L. (1976). Ethnic Self-Identity: Youth and Crisis. New York: Norton.

Duncan, B. and Duncan, O. (1968). Minorities and the Process of Stratification. *American Sociological Review, 33* (3). 356-364.

Eckland, B. (1979). Commentary and Debate. *Sociology of Education, 52.* 122-125.

Engelhart, M. (1972). *Methods of Educational Research.* Chicago: Rand McNally.

Erickson, E. (1968). *Identity: Youth and Crisis.* New York: Norton.

Erickson, F. (1987). Transformation and School Success: The Politics and Culture of Educational Achievement. *Anthropology and Education Quarterly, 18* (4). 335-356.

Espada, J. (1996). *Social Citizenship Rights.* Oxford: St. Anthony's College.

Evans, P., Rueschemeyer, D., and Skocpol, T. (1985). On the Road Toward a More Adequate Understanding of the State. In Evans, P., Rueschemeyer, D., and Skocpol, T. *Bringing the State Back In.* Cambridge: Cambridge University Press.

Fass, P. (1989). *Outside In: Minorities and the Transformation of American Education.* New York: Oxford University Press.

Fathi, A. (1972). Some Aspects of Changing Identity of Canadian Jewish Youth. *Jewish Social Studies, 34.* 3-30.

Featherman, D. & R. Hauser (1978). *Opportunity and Change.* New York: Academic Press.

Feinberg, W. and Soltis, J. (1998). *School and Society.* New York: Teachers College, Columbia University.

Fejgin, N. (1995). Factors Contributing to the Academic Excellence of American Jewish and Asian students. *Sociology of Education 68.* 18-30.

Fingers of Suspicion. (1992, April 25). *The Economist, 323* (7756).

Fitzgerald, C. (1962). Overseas Chinese in Southeast Asia. *Australian Journal of Politics and History, 8.* 66-77.

Fleming, J. (1984). *Blacks in College.* San Francisco: Jossey-Bass.

Fordham, S. and Ogbu, J. (1986). Black Students' School Success: Coping with the "Burden of 'Acting White'." *The Urban Review, 18* (3). 176-205.

Fordham, S. (1988). Racelessness as a Factor in Black Students' School Success:Pragmatic Strategy or Pyrrhic Victory? *Harvard Educational Review, 58* (l). 54-84.

Friendlier Neighbors. (1992, August 31). *Time, 140* (9).

Friends, Koreans, Countrymen. (1996, November 9). *The Economist, 341* (7991).

Giles, H., and Johnson, P. (1981). The Role of Language in Ethnic Group Relations. In Turner, C. and Giles, H. (Eds.). *Intergroup Behaviour.* Oxford: Blackwell.

Giles, H., Taylor, D., Lambert, W. & G. Albert (1979). Social Identity in Puerto Rico. *International Journal of Psychology, 14.* 185-201.

Giles, H., Llado, N., McKirnan, D. & D. Taylor (1976). Dimensions of Ethnic Identity:An Example from Northern Maine. *Journal of Social Psychology, 100.* 11-19.

Galston, W. (1993, Summer). *The Promise of Communitarianism, National Civic Review, 82.*

Gibson, M. (1987). The School Performance of Immigrant Minorities: A Comparative View. *Anthropology and Education Quarterly, 22* (1). 60-86.

Gibson, M. (1991). Minorities and Schooling: Some Implications. In Gibson, M. and Ogbu, J. (Eds.), *Minority Status and Schooling: A Comparative Study of Immigrant and Involuntary Minorities.* 357-381. New York: Garland.

Gordon, M. (1978). *Human Nature, Class and Ethnicity.* New York: Oxford University Press.

Gordon, M. (1964). *Assimilation in American Life.* New York: Oxford University Press

Gosling, P. (1983). Chinese Crop Dealers in Malaysia and Thailand: The Myth of the Merciless Monopsonistic Middleman. In Lim, L. and Gosling, P. (Ed.), *The Chinese in Southeast Asia, 1.* 131-170. Singapore: Maruzen Asia.

Gosling, P. (1983). Changing Chinese Identities in Southeast Asia: An Introductory Review. In Gosling P. and Lim, L. (Ed.), *The Chinese in Southeast Asia, 2.* 1-14. Singapore: Maruzen Asia.

Guskin, A. (1969). *Changing Identity: The Assimilation of Chinese in Thailand.* Unpublished Doctoral Dissertation, Ann Arbor, MI: University of Michigan.

Hafner, J. (1983). Market Gardening in Thailand: The Origins of an Ethnic Chinese Monopoly. In Lim, L. and Gosling, P. (Ed.), *The Chinese in Southeast Asia, 1.* 30-45. Singapore: Maruzen Asia.

Hearn, J. (1984). The Relative Roles of Academic, Ascribed, and Socioeconomic Characteristics in College Destination. *Sociology of Education, 57*. 22-30.

Hearn, J. (1991). Academic and Nonacademic Influences on the College Destinations of 1980 High School Graduates. *Sociology of Education, 54*. 157-71.

Hicks, G. and Mackie, J. (1994, July 14). A Question of Identity: Despite Media Hype, They are Firmly Settled in Southeast Asia. *Far Eastern Economics Review, 157* (28).

Hicks, G. and Mackie, J. (1994, July 14). Tension Persist: But Official Discrimination is on the Decline. *Far Eastern Economic Review, 157* (28).

Hobsbawm, (1993, December 16). The New Threat to History. *New York Review of Books*.

Hoffman, D. (1992, October-December). Changing Faces, Changing Places: The New Koreans in Japan. *Japan Quarterly, 39* (4).

Hoffman, D. (1996). Culture and Self in Multicultural Education: Reflections on Discourse, Text, and Practice. *American Educational Research Journal, 33* (3). 545-569.

Hofstede, G. (1980). *Culture's Consequences: International Differences in Work-Related Values*. Beverly Hills, CA: Sage.

Hossler, D. and Gallaher, K. (1987). Studying Students College Choice: A Three-Phase Model and the Implications for Policymakers. *College and University, 2*. 207-221.

Hossler, D., Braxton, J. and Coopersmith, G. (1989). Understanding Student College Choice. In J. Smart (Ed.), *Higher Education: Handbook of Theory and Research, 5*. 231-288. NY: Agathon Press.

Hui, C. and Triandis, H. (1986). Individualism-Collectivism: A Study of Cross-Cultural Researchers. *Journal of Cross-Cultural Psychology, 17*. 225-248.

Karen, D. (1988). Who Applies Where to College? Paper presented at the annual meeting of the American Educational Research Association, New Orleans.

Karen, D. (1990). Toward a Political-Organizational Model of Gatekeeping: The Case of Elite Colleges. *Sociology of Education, 63*. 227-240.

Kim, H. (1994, Summer). The Establishment of South Korean-Chinese Diplomatic Relations: A South Korean Perspective. *Journal of Northeast Asian Studies, 13* (2).

Klausen, J. (1995, January). Social Rights Advocacy and State Building: T.H. Marshall in the Hands of Social Reformers. *World Politics, 47* (2). 244-67.

Landa, J. (1983). The Political Economy of the Ethnically Homogeneous Chinese Middlemen Group in Southeast Asia:

Ethnicity and Entrepreneurship in a Plural Society. In Lim, L. and Gosling, P. (Ed.), *The Chinese in Southeast Asia, 1.* 86-116. Singapore: Maruzen Asia.

LeCompte, M., J. Preissle, & R. Tesch. (c1993). *Ethnography and Qualitative Design in Educational Research.* San Diego: Academic Press.

Lee, K. (1984). A *New History of Korea.* Cambridge, MA: Harvard University Press.

Lie, J. (1987, January). The Discriminated Fingers: The Korean Minority in Japan. *Monthly Review, 38.*

Lim, L. (1983). Chinese Business, Multinationals and the State Manufacturing for Export in Malaysia and Singapore. In Lim, L. and Gosling, P. (Ed.), *The Chinese in Southeast Asia, 1.* 245-274. Singapore: Maruzen Asia.

Lim, L. (1983). Chinese Economic Activity in Southeast Asia: An Introductory Review. In Lim, L. and Gosling, P. (Ed.), *The Chinese in Southeast Asia, 1.* 1-29. Singapore: Maruzen Asia.

Lim, M. (1983). The Ownership and Control of large Corporations in Malaysia: The Role of Chinese Businessmen. In Lim, L. and Gosling, P. (Ed.), *The Chinese in Southeast Asia, 1.* 275-315. Singapore: Maruzen Asia.

Limits of Family Values: Why the Overseas Chinese Have Done So Well, and Why They Need to Change. (1996, March 9). *The Economist, 338* (7956).

Lin, J. (1999). Social Transformation and Private Education in China. London: Prager.

Loh, K. (1983). The Transformation from Class to Ethnic Politics in an Opposition Area: A Malaysian Case Study. In Gosling, P. and Lim, L. (Ed.), *The Chinese in Southeast Asia, 2.* 189-214. Singapore: Maruzen Asia.

Mahihara, K. (1990, May 28). No Longer Willing to be Invisible. *Time, 135* (22).

Manski, C. and Wise, D. (1983). *College Choice in America.* Cambridge, MA: Harvard University Press.

Marshall, T. (1950/1992). *Citizenship and Social Class.* London: Pluto Press.

Marshall, T. & T. Bottomore (1992). *Citizenship and Social Class.* London: Pluto Press.

Massey, D. and Denton, N. (1993). *American Apartheid.* Cambridge, MA: Harvard University Press.

Masuda, M., Hasegawa, R., & G. Matsumoto (1973). The Ethnic Identity Questionnaire: A Comparison of Three Japanese Age Groups in Tachikawa, Japan, Honolulu, and Seattle. *Journal of Cross-Cultural Psychology, 4.* 229-244.

Masuda, M., Matsumoto, G., and Meredith, G. (1970). Salience of Ethnicity in the Spontaneous Self-Concept as a Function of One's Ethnic Distinctiveness in the Social Environment. *Journal of Personality and Social Psychology, 33.* 743-754.

Matute-Bianchi, M. (1991). Situational Ethnicity and Patterns of School PerformanceAiming Immigrant and Nonimmigrant Mexican-Descent Students. In Gibson, M.and Ogbu, J. (Eds.). *Minority Status and Schooling: A Comparative Study of Immigrant and Involuntary Minorities.* 205-247. New York: Garland Press.

McCarthy, C. (1993). Beyond the Poverty of Theory in Race Relations: Non Synchrony and Social Difference in Education. In Weiss, L. and Fine, M. (Eds) *Beyond Silenced Voices.* Albany, NY: State University of New York Press.

McDonough, P., Korn, J., and Yamasaki, E. (1997). Admission Advantage for Sale: Private College Counselors and the Students Who Use Them. *Review of Higher Education, 20.* 297-317.

McDonough, P. (1997). *Choosing Colleges: How Social Class and Schools Structure Opportunity.* Albany, NY: State University of New York Press.

McGuire, J., McGuire, C. Child, P. and Fujioka, T. (1978). Salience of Ethnicity in the Spontaneous Self-Concept as a Function on One's Ethnic Distinctiveness in the Social Environment. *Journal of Personality and Social Psychology, 36* (5). 511-520.

Merriam, S. (1998). *Qualitative Research and Case Study Applications in Education.* San Francisco: Jossey-Bass.

Min, P. (1992, Spring). A Comparison of the Korean Minorities in China and Japan. *International Migration Review, 26* (1).

Ministry of Justice, Republic of Korea (1996). *Annual Report of Statistics on Legal Migration, 1996.*

Nagel, J. (1994, February). Constructing Ethnicity: Creating and Recreating Ethnic Identity and Culture. *Social Problems, 41* (1). 152-76.

Nonini, D. (1983). The Chinese Truck Transport "Industry" of a Peninsular Malaysia Market Town. In Lim, L. and. Gosling, P. (Ed.), *The Chinese in Southeast Asia, 1.* 1-29. Singapore: Maruzen Asia.

Oakes, J. and Lipton, M. (1992). Detracking Schools: Early Lessons from the Field. *Phi Delta Kappan, 73* (6). 448-454.

Okamura, J. (1981). *Situational Ethnicity. Ethnic and Racial Studies,* 4 (4). 452-465.

O'Keefe, J. (1993). Working Toward an Inclusive School Culture: A University- Secondary School Collaborative Model of Reflective Practice. Orlando FL: Address delivered at the annual meeting of the American Association of School Administrators. (*ERIC Document Reproduction Service* No. ED 378 678).

Ogbu, J. (1987/1991). Immigrant and Involuntary Minorities in Comparative Perspective. In Gibson, M. and Ogbu, J. (Eds.). *Minority Status and Schooling: A Comparative Study of Immigrant and Involuntary Minorities*. 3-33. New York: Garland Press.

Ogbu, J. and Simons, D. (1998). Voluntary and Involuntary Minorities: A Cultural-Ecological Theory of School Performance with Some Implications for Education. *American Anthropological Association, 29* (2). 155-188.

Olneck, M. (1979). The Effects of Education. In Jencks, C., et al. *Who Gets Ahead?: The Determinants of Economic Success in America*. 159-190. NY: Basic Books.

Olneck, M. (1989). Americanization and the Education of Immigrants: An Analysis of Symbolic Action. *American Journal of Education, 97* (4). 398-423.

Olneck, M. (1990). The Recurring Dream: Symbolism and Ideology in Intercultural Education and Multicultural Education. *American Journal of Education, 98* (2). 147-174.

Omohundro, J. (1983). Social Network and Business Success for the Philippine Chinese. In Lim, L. and Gosling, P. (Ed.), *The Chinese in Southeast Asia, 1*. 65-85. Singapore: Maruzen Asia.

Ortiz, F. (1988). "Hispanic-American Children's Experiences in Classrooms: A Comparison Between Hispanic and Non-Hispanic Children." In Weis, L. (Ed.) *Class, Race and Gender in American Education*. Albany: State University of New York Press.

Overseas Chinese: A Driving Force. (1992, July 18). *The Economist, 324* (7768).

Paisley, E., Kaye, L. and Baum, J. (1992, September 3). Risks and Rewards. *Far Eastern Economic Review, 155* (35).

Pan, L. (1994, July 14). Ersatz Chinese? *Far Eastern Economic Review*, 157(28).

Palmier, L. (1960). *Social Status and Power in Java*. London: The Athlone Press.

Park, E. (1986). *The Ethnicity of the Chinese in Korea*. Seoul: Korea Research Center.

Pang, E. (1983). Race, Income Distributions, and Development in Malaysia and Singapore. In Lim, L. and Gosling, P. (Ed.), *The Chinese in Southeast Asia, 1*. 316-335. Singapore: Maruzen Asia.

Perlmann, J. (1988). *Ethnic Differences: Schooling and Social Structure Among the Irish, Italians, Jews and Blacks in an American City, 1880-1935*. New York: Cambridge University Press.

Pervin, L. (1968). Performance and Satisfaction As a Function of Individual-Environment Fit. *Psychological Bulletin, 69* (1). 56-58.

Phinney, J. (1996, November-December). Understanding Ethnic Diversity: The Role of Ethnic Identity. *American Behavioral Scientist, 40* (2).

Pipes, M., Westby, C., and Inglebret, E. (1993). *Faculty and Student Challenges in Facing Cultural and Linguistic Diversity.* Springfield, IL: Charles C. Thomas. Press.

Poston Jr., M., Mao, M., and Yu, M. (1994, September). The Global Distribution of the Overseas Chinese Around 1990. *Population and Development Review, 20* (3).

Portes, A. and Rumbaut, R. (1990). *Immigrant America: A Portrait.* Berkeley: University of California Press.

Purcell, V. (1948). *The Chinese in Malaya.* London: Oxford University Press.

Purcell, V. (1960). *The Chinese in Modern Malaya.* (2nd rev. ed.) Singapore: Donald Moore.

Purcell, V. (1965). *The Chinese in Southeast Asia.* (2nd ed.) London: Oxford University Press.

Pye, L. (1954). *Some Observations on the Political Behavior of Overseas Chinese.* Cambridge, MA: MIT Press.

Pye, L. (1956). *Guerrilla Communism in Malaya.* London: Oxford University Press.

Ravitch, D. (1974). The Great School Wars. New York: Basic Books.

Raybeck, D. (1983). Chinese Patterns of Adaptation in Southeast Asia. In Gosling, P. and Lim, L. (Ed.), *The Chinese in Southeast Asia, 2.* 15-33. Singapore: Maruzen Asia.

Richardson, J., Simmons, H. and de los Santos, A. (1987). Graduating Minority Students. *Change, 19* (3). 20-27.

Rogler, L., Cooney, R., and Ortiz, V. (1980). Intergenerational Change in Ethnic Identity in the Puerto Rican Family. *International Migration Review, 14.* 193-214.

Rosenthal. D., Bell, R., Demetriou, A., and Efklindes, A. (1989). From Collectivism to Individualism? The Acculturation of Greek Immigrants in Australia. *International Journal of Behavioral Development, 24.* 57-71.

Rosenthal, D. & A. Cichello (1986). The Meeting of Two Cultures: Ethnic Identity and Psychosocial Adjustment of Italian-Australian Adolescents. *International Journal of Psychology, 21.* 487-501.

Rosenthal D. and Feldman, S. (1992). The nature and stability of ethnic identity in Chinese Youth. *Journal of Cross-Cultural Psychology, 23* (2). 214-227.

Rosenthal D. & C. Hrynevich (1987). The Dynamic Nature of Ethnic Identity Among Greek-Australian Adolescents. *Journal of Social Psychology, 129.* 249-258.

Rubin, H. & I. Rubin. (1995). *Qualitative Interviewing: The Art of Hearing Data*. London: SAGE Publications.

Rumbaut, R. (1994). The Crucible Within: Ethnic Identity, Self-Esteem, and Segmented Assimilation Among Children of Immigrants. *International Migration Review, 28* (4). 748-794.

Schurenberg, E. (1989, May). *The Agony of College Admissions*. Money Magazine.142-66.

Scourby, A. (1980). Three Generations of Greek Americans: A Study in Ethnicity. International Migration Review, 14. 43-52.

Semons, M. (1991). Naturalistic Study of Student Experiences. *The Urban Review, 23* (3). 137-157.

Shim, J. (1992, October 8). Identity Crisis: Chinese Residents Split Over Switch to Peking. *Far Eastern Economic Review, 155* (40).

Silverman, D. (ed.) (1997). *Qualitative Research: Theory, Method and Practice*. London: SAGE Publications.

Siow, M. (1983). The Problem of Ethnic Cohesion Among the Chinese in Peninsular Malaysia: Intraethnic Divisions and Interethnic Accommodations. In Gosling, P. and Lim, L. (Ed.), *The Chinese in Southeast Asia, 2*. 170-188. Singapore: Maruzen Asia.

Skinner, W. (1960). Change and Persistence in Chinese Culture Overseas: A Comparison of Thailand and Java. *Journal of the South Sea Society, 16*. 86-100.

Skinner, G. W. (1957). *Chinese Society in Thailand: An Analytical History*. Ithaca, NY: Cornell University Press.

Skinner, G. (1964). The Thailand Chinese: Assimilation in Changing Society. *Asia, 2*. 80-82

Sleeter, C. and Grant, C. (1985). Race, Class, and Gender in an Urban School. *Urban Education, 20* (1). 37-60.

Smedley, B., Myers, H. and Shelly, H. (1993). Minority-Status Stresses and the College Adjustment of Ethnic Minority Freshman. *Journal of Higher Education, 64* (4).434-453.

Smith, T. (1969, Fall). Immigrant Social Aspirations and American Education, 1880-1930. *American Quarterly, 21* (3). 523-543.

Stanford, M. (1994). *A Companion to the Study of History*. Cambridge, MA: Blackwell.

Strauch, J. (1983). The Political Economy of a Chinese-Malaysian New Village: Highly Diversified Insecurity. In Lim, L. and Gosling, P. (Ed.), *The Chinese in Southeast Asia, 1*. 207-231. Singapore: Maruzen Asia.

Stanlaw, J. and Peshkin, A. (1988). Black Visibility in a Multiethnic High School. In Weis, L. (Ed.) *Class, Race and Gender in American Education*. Albany: State University of New York Press.

Tan, C. (1983). Acculturation and the Chinese in Melaka: The Expression of Baba Identity Today. Gosling, P. and Lim, L. (Ed.), *The Chinese in Southeast Asia, 1.* 56-78. Singapore: Maruzen Asia.

Tan. C. (1988). *The Baba of Melaka: Culture and Identity of a Chinese Peranakan Community in Malaysia.* Petaling Jaya, Selangor: Pelanduk Publications.

Tan, C. (1992). *Bibliography on Ethnic Relations with Special Reference to Malaysia and Singapore.* Kuala Lumpur: Institute of Advanced Studies, University of Malaysia.

Tan, C. (1993). *Chinese Peranakan Heritage in Malaysia* and Singapore. Kuala Lumpur: Fajar Bakti

Terra, D. (1983). The Effects of Language Planning on a Penang Hokkien Kampong: People Separated by a Blade of Grass Could Not Understand Each Other. In Gosling, P. and Lim, L. (Ed.), *The Chinese in Southeast Asia, 2.* 126-146. Singapore: Maruzen Asia.

Tesche, A. (1974). The Native American experience. (Report No. 1). Davis: University of California. (*ERIC Document Reproduction Service* No. ED 156 067).

Thomas, G. (1979). The Influence of Ascription, Achievement, and Educational Expectations on Black-White Postsecondary Enrollment. *The Sociological Quarterly, 20.* 209-222.

Thompson, F. (1920). *Schooling of the Immigrant.* New York: Harper & Brothers.

Thomson, C. (1993, October). Political Identity Among Chinese in Thailand. *The Geographical Review, 83* (4). 397-409.

Ting-Toomey, S. (1981). Ethnic Identity and Close Friendship in Chinese-American College Students. *International Journal of Intercultural Relations, 5.* 383-406.

Tinto, V. (1975). Dropout from Higher Education: A Theoretical Synthesis of Recent Research. *Review of Educational Research, 45.* 89-125.

Tolor, A. (ed.) (1985). Effective Interviewing. Springfield, IL: Charles C. Thomas.

Tyack,D. (1993). Constructing Difference: Historical Reflections on Schooling and Social Diversity. *Teachers College Record 95* (l). 8-34.

Vanishing of Chinatown: South Korea. (1996, August 3). *The Economist, 340* (7977).

Vatikiotis, M. (1996, Jan.). Sino Chic; Suddenly, It's Cool to be Chinese. *Far Eastern Economic Review, 159* (2).

Vermeulen, H. and Pels, T. (1984). Ethnic Identity and Young Migrants in the Netherlands. *Prospects, 16* (2). 277-282.

Wang, G. (1981). *Community and Nation: Essays on Southeast Asia and the Chinese.* Kuala Lumpur; Hong Kong: Heinmann Educational Books (Asia) Ltd.

Weber, M. (1920, c1978). *Economy and Society*. Berkeley, CA: University of California Press.

Weidenbaum, M. and Hughes, S. (1996, September-October). Asia's Bamboo Network. *The American Enterprise, 7* (5).

Weidenbaum, M. (1996, September 1). The Bamboo Network: Overseas Chinese Commercial Families. *Vital Speeches, 62* (22).

Weinberg, M. (1977). *A Chance to Learn*. Cambridge, MA: Cambridge University Press.

Williams, L. (1960). *Overseas Chinese Nationalism: The Genesis of the Pan-Chinese Movements in Indonesia, 1900-1916*. The Center for International Studies, Massachusetts Institute of Technology. Glencoe, Ill.: The Free Press.

Williams, L. (1966). *The Future of the Overseas Chinese in Southeast Asia*. New York: McGraw-Hill.

Williams, L. (1967). The Overseas Chinese and Peking. *Trans-Action, 4* (3). 5-9.

Willmott, D. (1960). *The Chinese of Semarang: A Changing Minority Community in Indonesia*. Ithaca, NY: Cornell University Press.

Wilmer, F. (1997, Summer). Identity, Culture and Historicity: The Social Construction of Ethnicity in the Balkans. *World Affairs, 160* (1).

Winzeler, R. (1983). The Ethnic Status of the Rural Chinese of the Kelantan Plain. In Gosling, P. & L. Lim (Ed.), *The Chinese in Southeast Asia, 2*. 34-55. Singapore: Maruzen Asia.

Wooden, W., Leon, J., and Toshima, E. (1988). Ethnic Identity Among Sansei and Yonsei Church-Affiliated Youth in Los Angeles and Honolulu. *Psychological Reports, 62*. 268-270.

Wright, C. (1993). School Processes - An Ethnographic Study. In Woods, P. and Hammersley, M. (Eds.) *Gender and Ethnicity in Schools*. New York: Routleage.

Yengoyan, A. (1983). The Buying of Futures: Chinese Merchants and the Fishing Industry in Capiz, Philippines. In Lim, L. and Gosling, P. (Ed.), *The Chinese in Southeast Asia, 1*. 117-130. Singapore: Maruzen Asia.

Yin, R. (c1994). Case Study Research: Design and Methods. *Applied Social Research Methods Series, 5*. Thousand Oaks; London; New Delhi: SAGE Publications.

Zabrovkaia, L. (1993, Spring). Consequences of Korean Emigration to Jiandao. *Korea Journal, 33* (1).

Zimmermann, K. and Bauer, T. (1997). Network Migration of Ethnic Germans. *International Migration Review*.

Index